What the Bible teaches about

The Person of Christ

Stuart Olyott

EP BOOKS
1st Floor Venture House, 6 Silver Court, Watchmead,
Welwyn Garden City, UK, AL7 1TS

web: http://www.epbooks.org

e-mail: sales@epbooks.org

EP Books are distributed in the USA by:
JPL Distribution
3741 Linden Avenue Southeast
Grand Rapids, MI 49548
E-mail: orders@jpldistribution.com
Tel: 877.683.6935

© Stuart Olyott 2000. All rights reserved. No part of this publication may be reproduced, stored in a retrieval system or transmitted, in any form, or by any means, electronic, mechanical, photocopying, recording or otherwise, without the prior permission of the publishers.

Released as *Jesus is both God and Man* in 2000
This edition 2016

British Library Cataloguing in Publication Data available

ISBN 978–1–78397–156–5

All Scripture quotations, unless otherwise indicated, are taken from the **New King James Version**. Copyright © 1982 by Thomas Nelson, Inc. Used by permission. All rights reserved. Printed and bound in Great Britain by Creative Print & Design Wales, Ebbw Vale.

To
Ernest A. Cresswell,
Church Secretary of Belvidere Road Church, Liverpool, 1955–1982, with thanks to God for your spiritual example, wisdom, courage and fellowship in upholding the truth of the gospel.

Who is this?

Who is this, so weak and helpless,
Child of lowly Hebrew maid,
Rudely in a stable sheltered,
Coldly in a manger laid?
'Tis the Lord of all creation,
Who this wondrous path hath trod;
He is God from everlasting,
And to everlasting God.

Who is this, a Man of Sorrows,
Walking sadly life's hard way,
Homeless, weary, sighing, weeping
Over sin and Satan's sway?
'Tis our God, our glorious Saviour,
Who above the starry sky
Now for us a place prepareth,
Where no tear can dim the eye.

Who is this? Behold him shedding
Drops of blood upon the ground!
Who is this, despised, rejected,
Mocked, insulted, beaten, bound?
'Tis our God, who gifts and graces
On his church now poureth down;

Who shall smite in holy vengeance
All his foes beneath his throne.

Who is this that hangeth dying
While the rude world scoffs and scorns,
Numbered with the malefactors,
Torn with nails, and crowned with thorns?
'Tis the God who ever liveth
'Mid the shining ones on high,
In the glorious golden city,
Reigning everlastingly.

William Walsham How,
1823–1897.

Contents

	Page
Foreword	9
Preface	13
The Lord—his deity	15
Introduction	17
1. Eternally God	19
2. God with us	33
3. God—now and always	55
Jesus—his humanity	71
4. The promise of a man	73
5. Behold the man!	83
6. A man now and for ever	101

Christ—his unipersonality   113

7. One person   115

8. Two distinct natures   127

9. Heresies, ancient and modern   139

    Postscript   159

    Appendix 1 The Creed of Chalcedon   161

    Appendix 2 The Athanasian Creed   163

    Scripture Index   167

Foreword

It was not long ago that modernization, in its relentless march, seemed poised to strip western societies of all vestiges of religion. Certainly, Europe seems to offer first-hand evidence of this reversal. The more its societies become urbanized, the more completely capitalism drives their preoccupations; the more laced together they are by technology, and the more pervasive are the means of mass communication, the less religious they become. Many of its magnificent cathedrals are virtually empty on Sunday. They are visited more by sightseers than worshippers. They stand as monuments to a bygone age of faith which has now withered under the high noon of modernity. And it is not only the cathedrals that are empty—so, too, are many churches. In fact, in France there are more witches and fortune tellers than there are clergy.

The American picture

In America, however, the picture is dramatically different. Undoubtedly it is a showcase of what a modern society looks like with its unparalleled abundance, its ubiquitous technology, its large and productive cities, its extraordinary research facilities which day after day produce new discoveries in the far-off galaxies, as well as in the smallest particles of matter. But, at the same time, Americans are now becoming preoccupied with the spiritual. It is a strange and unexpected turn of events. The complete secularization of life which was being so confidently predicted in the 1970s has, instead, turned into a search for what is non-material in life, for mystery, for what is not rational. To be sure, this spirituality comes in many forms and, given the highly therapeutic culture in which we live, much of it seems to be inwardly directed to finding meaning and morality in the self, that was once found outside the self in God, or his Christ, or his Word. This is not so much the kind of pilgrimage on which Christian sets out in John Bunyan's *Pilgrim's Progress* in which, despite the multitude of difficulties which he encounters and the mistakes which he makes, in the end he always comes to his senses: he is a child of God and he knows towards whom he is journeying. When he crosses the river of Jordan at death, there is no doubt that it will be the Lord who meets him on the other side. This modern spiritual journey is, by contrast, quite different. The destination is unknown; the interest is in the search, not the discovery; it is a search through the self, conducted through the self so what is intuitive and irrational are a central part of this spirituality. What seems to have happened then is that the experience of modernity has turned the search for what is spiritual inward, into the self; and yet the very emptiness to which this search attests is surely evidence of the fact that, as made in the image of God, we are restless until we have found our rest in God.

Moral relativism

This sudden change in cultural mood, from hard-edged secularism ten and twenty years ago to this soft, therapeutic pursuit of reality, has spilled over in many directions. One of the most important, of course, is that it has fuelled the fires of relativism. In America, 67% do not believe in moral absolutes and 70% do not believe in absolute truth. It is the relativists who constitute America's moral majority. We are a nation which is building a brilliant and ingenious civilization, but it is being built over a moral and spiritual vacuum. The modesty which should moderate our ambition has been perverted and is, instead, consuming our faculty of knowing. We are so uncertain of our place in reality, so dislocated from the moral world which we once inhabited that we have come to think that it is of the essence of honesty, not to say sophistication, to claim that we can know nothing certain at all, that all knowledge must be revised in the light of our experience, that in the centre of life there are no fixed and unchanging truths.

On the face of it, this seems like a completely novel situation. But we would be quite mistaken to think that pluralism is an invention of the late twentieth century. The truth is that the very first Christian believers walked a world that was filled with thousands of gods and goddesses. It was a highly pluralistic world though its causes were quite different from those that drive our pluralism today. Then, the proclamation of Christ as uniquely divine and as alone true was awkwardly countercultural, as it is now. Then it flew in the face of cultural habits which were deep and entrenched; and it does now. Yet it was this proclamation which, we know, turned the world upside down, and by the third century led Tertullian to say that the Christians had left the pagans nothing but their empty temples.

Preservation of the truth

Of course, matters were not quite as simple as this might suggest. While the church marched forward with the truth of Christ, it also had to fight a tenacious rearguard action to preserve the truths of his full divinity, full humanity in one person. From within the church, there arose those who doubted his full divinity and others who doubted his full humanity. If there were those who divided his person, there were those who confused it. Some diluted the biblical testimony to Christ; others sought to add to it; and still others sought to subtract from it. At the Council of Chalcedon in 451, the church asserted definitively, in a crystal clear way, its doctrine of the two natures in one person. After more than a century of painful, intense debate, this must have seemed like the end of a long journey. And so it was—for a while. But in the late twentieth century, it is safe to say, most christological thinking in the academic world has begun with the premise that Chalcedon must be rejected. What was gained by the almost heroic action of some of the early fathers has been jettisoned by the learned who dominate the postmodern academic guild. This loss raises a perplexing question. How can Christian faith survive in the absence of a Christ who is uniquely God incarnate? What gospel do we have left to proclaim to a world that is replete with consumer goods but painfully adrift on the high seas of modernity, if it does not have at its heart the substitutionary death of Christ? The awkwardness of this countercultural message is precisely its glory, not its undoing.

Stuart Olyott's *Jesus is both God and man* is a sure-footed study of what the Bible teaches about Christ. In addition to its clarity, which is no mean virtue these days, what stands out is the spirit in which it is written. This is the work of a 'kneeling theologian'. This is an author who has a keen sense of the majesty of the Christ about whom he is writing, who knows that first our thoughts about Christ must be biblically ordered and then our hearts must be humbled before him. This is no mere academic excursion. It is a summons to believe right, and to live well, in the presence of the Christ who inhabits eternity, who holds the worlds in his hand, who upholds everything by his power, and towards whom all life is moving, for one day he will come in awesome power and judgement. This is a book well worth reading and pondering.

David E Wells

Academic Dean
Gordon-Conwell Theological Seminary, Charlotte

Preface

This book is not a summary of the life of the Lord Jesus Christ. Nor does it examine what he came on earth to do. It is a look at his glorious person. It studies what the Bible says about *who he is*.

There are many reasons why such a book as this is needed. One springs from the rise of the modern cults. Our homes are frequently visited by those who teach things about the Lord Jesus Christ which are far less glorious than what the Scriptures teach. We cannot bear to see him so publicly degraded, and need to learn how to answer these false teachers convincingly.

Then there is the need of young Christians who, largely because of poor teaching in the churches, are very confused about what God has revealed concerning his Son. It is from the ranks of these new converts that our future Christian leaders will come. It is therefore supremely important that they should learn to uphold clearly the glories of the Lord Jesus Christ in this world.

But there is a reason for this book which is greater than all the others. What the Scriptures teach about the person of our Saviour is so high and glorious that it can evoke nothing but adoring wonder from those who love him. We spend too little time merely contemplating him. The spirit of devotion is dying among us. The mystery no longer awes us. The Trinity is the first great mystery of being, and the person of our Lord is the second. When we consider him afresh, we fall at his feet to worship him. We are truly 'lost in wonder, love and praise'.

If this little book causes some child of God to seek a quiet place and there, in holy adoration, to enjoy the company of the Lord Jesus Christ, it will have served the real purpose for which it was written.

Jesus! my Shepherd, Saviour, Friend;
My Prophet, Priest and King;
My Lord, my Life, my Way, my End:
Accept the praise I bring.

Stuart Olyott

The Lord—his deity

Introduction

What the Bible teaches about the person of the Lord Jesus Christ is summed up in his name.

He is *the Lord*, the self-existent and self-sufficient God. He is *Jesus*, his human name reminding us that he became man and that to this day he has a real human nature. He is *Christ*, the 'anointed one', the Messiah—not two persons, but one.

These are the three facts that we must keep in our minds whenever we think of him. The use of his name helps us to do so. The three sections of our book, each composed of three chapters, look at these themes in turn.

1

Eternally God

If Christ is not God, then we who worship him are idolaters. However, if he is God and we fail to worship him, we are the worst rebels of all.

If Christ is not God, he was a blasphemer, a fake and an impostor. We cannot even accept him as a good man, because his claims to deity were clear. However, if he is God, but we talk of him only as a good man, it is *we* who are the blasphemers.

There is no question so crucial and as far-reaching as this one: who is Jesus? Is he, or is he not, God? What do the Scriptures teach?

Pre-existent

The Bible's teaching is that Jesus Christ existed before his conception and birth. His birth did not mark his origin, but only his appearance as a man on the stage of history. Throughout his earthly life he displayed a consciousness of his previous existence. 'I came forth from the Father,' he said, 'and have come into the world' (John 16:28). He described himself as 'he who came down from heaven (John 3:13), and asked his hearers what they would think if they saw him 'ascend where he was before' (John 6:62). That these public statements were an accurate reflection of his deepest consciousness is proved by his personal prayer to God: 'And now, O Father, glorify me together with yourself, with the glory which I had with you before the world was' (John 17:5). The inspired writers of the Scriptures saw Jesus as he saw himself. He is the one who is 'from the beginning' (1 John 1:1), 'in the beginning' (John 1:1) and 'before all things' (Colossians 1:17). He was in the world, not as one with a normal human origin, but as 'he who comes from above … he who comes from heaven (John 3:31). Before he entered into the poverty of his human life 'he was rich' (2 Corinthians 8:9). Of course he was! This man was none other than 'the Lord from heaven' (1 Corinthians 15:47). It was because he recognized Christ's true identity that John the Baptist could say of the one born after him, 'He who comes after me is preferred before me, for he was before me' (John 1:15,30).

Pre-existent as God

No student of Scripture can fail to be convinced of the pre-existence of Christ. But many have been slow to see that pre-existence implies deity. This was the mistake of the Arians who caused so much difficulty in the early centuries of the Christian church. They were willing to accept Christ's pre-existence, but still saw him only as the greatest of all creatures, through whom God created everything else. They could not accept that his pre-existence was *eternal*. To them he was simply the greatest creature God had made, and more like God than anything else in existence. But because he himself was created, he could not be God in the same sense as the Father was.

Nearer the truth, but still far from it, were the so-called Semi-Arians. They accepted Christ as eternal, and denied that he was a creature. But they could not bring themselves to believe that he was as much God as the Father was.

Christ's own testimony

In stark contrast to these views stand the statements of Christ himself. 'Before Abraham was, I AM,' he said (John 8:58). This was not just a simple statement of pre-existence. He could have made that by declaring, 'Before Abraham was, I was.' His 'I AM' was a claim to a continued and ever-present existence from before Abraham's time to the moment he was speaking. Indeed, it is the language of self-existence. Jesus Christ's own claim to pre-existence was also a claim to deity. This was well understood by the Jews who were listening, especially as they knew 'I AM' to be God's description of himself. To them Christ's words were open blasphemy, and their response to them was to take up stones to stone him. They could never have done this if they had put an Arian or Semi-Arian interpretation on his statement.

Pre-existence and deity are also linked together in the mind of the apostle John at the very beginning of his Gospel. The profound words which open it are well known: 'In the beginning was the Word, and the Word was with God, and the Word was God. He was in the beginning with God. All things were made through him, and without him nothing was made that was made' (John 1:1–3).

These words are worthy of our closest attention. They clearly teach that when things began to come into being, he already *was*. Jesus Christ had no beginning. If he did, how could he possibly have been present 'in the beginning'? Equally clearly, these verses teach that he is not a creature. If he was a creature in any sense it would not be true that 'without him nothing was made that was made'. The Word was without beginning and unmade. We can never again countenance the errors of the Arians.

John says that this eternal Unmade was eternally with God. But this does not mean that he was less than God, as the Semi-Arians contend. 'The Word *was* God.' John is as dogmatic as that about the deity of Christ, and his words stand as a perpetual contradiction of the Semi-Arian position. There is no way to dismiss these words, or to evade their full impact. Indeed, the way in which John arranges his words in the original Greek (with the predicate preceding the subject) means that he is actually *stressing* the full deity of Christ. It would be perfectly legitimate to render his words, 'And the Word was God *himself*'!

Other New Testament teaching

Of course, all this is very confusing to the human mind. How can the Word *be* God, and yet be *with* God? To answer this question we would have to look at the doctrine of the Trinity, which is beyond the scope of this book.[1] But the facts stated by John should be noted. We cannot understand *how* these things can be so, but it would be a serious mistake to let the poverty of our understanding pervert John's statements. *What* he is saying is clear enough, and it does not allow us to fall into the errors we have mentioned.

There are many other passages in the New Testament which carry the same teaching as John's classic statement. An important one is Philippians 2:5-11, and verses 5-7 are especially relevant at this point. Paul clearly teaches that Christ had a pre-incarnate state before he came among us as a man. In that state he had, by right, equality with God, but did not consider this something to cling to. Instead he laid aside the divine majesty, assumed human nature in the form of a servant and became obedient in action and suffering to the point where he died a shameful death. In doing so he set us an example of self-effacement which the apostle calls on us to follow. As countless exegetes have shown, every word which Paul uses rules out Arian and Semi-Arian understandings of Christ's pre-incarnate state. Paul's whole appeal is based on the fact of the immensity of the condescension of Christ. He who is by inalienable right the eternal Son of God became man!

Another striking passage on the same theme is Hebrews 1:1-3. Christ's pre-existence is there proved by the simple statement that it was by him that God made the universe. This pre-existent Christ is then said to be the brightness of God's glory and the express image of his person. But what does *that* mean?

This means that all the brightness of God's glory shines forth from his Son. His was no lesser glory, but 'humble as was the external appearance of Jesus of Nazareth, He was the true Shekinah, in whom dwelt the Godhead bodily—the real, substantial, adequate representation of the King eternal, immortal and invisible, whom no eye hath seen, or can see' (John Brown). The Lord Jesus Christ is the perfect picture of what God is like. He is the very impress of his substance. God is perfectly revealed to us through him who said, 'He who has seen me has seen the Father' (John 14:9). The mystery baffles us, but we cannot deny it because of that. The pre-existent Creator, who is distinct from the Father, is no one less than God himself!

Called God

Some people express surprise when we go so far as actually to call the Lord Jesus Christ 'God'. They treat the opening verses of John's Gospel, which we looked at in the paragraphs above, as if they were exceptional or unusual. But this is not so. The names and titles of God are frequently given to the Lord Jesus Christ in Scripture.

A good example is the word found in our Bibles as 'LORD'. The Old Testament was written in Hebrew, and the word used for 'LORD' was the word most familiarly known to us as *Jehovah*. But the time came when most Jews could no longer read Hebrew. It became necessary to translate the Old Testament into Greek, which they readily understood. In the translation, better known as the Septuagint, the word *Jehovah* was usually rendered by the Greek word *kyrios*, as were two other divine titles. *Kyrios* quickly became the most commonly used word for God. When the New Testament came to be written, it was precisely this word which was applied to our Lord Jesus Christ, and which is rendered 'LORD' in most of our English versions. The word used for Jehovah is the word used for the Lord Jesus Christ! (See Matthew 7:22; Luke 2:11, 5:8; John 20:28; 1 Corinthians 12:3; 2 Peter 3:2,18).

This need surprise us only if we do not believe that Christ is the eternal God. As it is, the writer to the Hebrews refers the words, 'Your throne, O God, is for ever and ever' to the Lord

Jesus Christ (Psalm 45:6-7; Hebrews 1:8). This is but one of many occasions where Old Testament passages which referred to Jehovah are applied to Christ by the New Testament writers. By looking at these passages we can quickly see that it is proper to speak of Christ as 'God' (Numbers 21:5-6; 1 Corinthians 10:9); 'My God ... you are the same, and your years will have no end' (Psalm 102:24-27; Hebrews 1:10-12); 'the King, the LORD of hosts' (Isaiah 6:1-10; John 12:39-41); 'the LORD of hosts himself' (Isaiah 8:13-14, (AV); Romans 9:33); '[the] Mighty God' (Isaiah 9:1-6; Matthew 4:14-16) and 'the Lord' (Malachi 3:1; Matthew 11:10).

In the same vein Paul is not ashamed to call him 'Christ ... who is over all, the eternally blessed God' (Romans 9:5) and 'our great God and Saviour' (Titus 2:13, a verse where we need to notice carefully that Paul is speaking of only one person, and not two). To John he is 'the Alpha and the Omega ... the Almighty' (Revelation 1:8), and he unambiguously assures us that 'This is the true God and eternal life' (1 John 5:20).

Evidently God

The Scriptures will simply not permit us to think less of Christ than we ought to. They will not allow us to miss the point. When we see him as the pre-incarnate Son of God, who is actually called God, we have not exhausted the biblical data. Divine attributes are ascribed to him. He did divine works and received divine worship. We now look at each of these points in turn, all the while remembering that at this stage in our book we are looking at our Lord *before* he came among us as a man.

One of the attributes of God is eternity. This is quite clearly ascribed to the Lord Jesus Christ in Scripture. For instance, in Isaiah 44:6 we read of Jehovah saying, 'I am the first and I am the last.' Yet in Revelation, Jesus says, 'I am the Alpha and the Omega, the beginning and the end, the first and the last' (Revelation 22:13). Jehovah is eternal; Jesus is eternal. Clearly Jesus is Jehovah: he is God.

In the same way we know that God is immutable (Malachi 3:6). He is always the same. He cannot change. But what is true of God alone is true of the Lord Jesus Christ. We can say to him, 'You are the same' (Hebrews 1:12). We are comforted by knowing him as 'Jesus Christ ... the same yesterday, today, and for ever' (Hebrews 13:8).

It is not surprising that he who is called God, and who has divine attributes, is seen doing divine works even before his incarnation. The Bible opens with the simply magnificent words: 'In the beginning God created the heavens and the earth' (Genesis 1:1). But it also leaves us in no doubt that Jesus Christ is the Creator, and that 'All things were made through him, and without him nothing was made that was made ... the world was made through him ...' 'By him all things were created ... All things were created through him and for him' (John 1:3,10; Colossians 1:16–17). It is to Christ that the following words are addressed: 'You, LORD, in the beginning laid the foundation of the earth, and the heavens are the work of your hands; they will perish, but you remain' (Hebrews 1:10–11).

God's rule

But did God create his world, and then leave it to function without him? Not at all. He personally rules and directs what he has made. 'His kingdom rules over all'; 'His tender mercies are over all his works' (Psalm 103:19; 145:9). Yet it is by Jesus that 'all things consist' (Colossians 1:17). He is the one 'upholding all things by the word of his power' (Hebrews 1:3). It is he who has ruled creation from its beginning to this present moment. Who but God can do the works of God?

These things being so, we would expect worship to be given to the pre-incarnate Christ, and this is exactly what we find. In Isaiah chapter 6 we read of a wonderful incident which took place about 700 BC. In the temple the prophet Isaiah had a vision of Jehovah. He saw him on his throne, as the very centre of the adoration of heaven. Surrounding him were the glorious seraphim who, although they themselves are sinless, could not look on his unblemished majesty. 'Holy, holy, holy is the Lord of hosts,' they called, 'the whole earth is full of his glory!' (Isaiah 6:3). The whole building trembled at this truth, and was filled with smoke. The watching prophet was entirely overcome by what he saw and was filled with a sense of defilement and pollution as he contrasted his own sin with what he was witnessing.

In his Gospel, John tells us that what Isaiah saw was the glory of the Lord Jesus Christ! Quoting from what Jehovah had said to the ancient prophet at that moment, he adds, 'These things Isaiah said when he saw his glory and spoke of him' (John 12:41). It is evident from the immediate context that the 'his' and 'him' are references to the Lord Jesus Christ (see vv. 37–41). The Jehovah that Isaiah saw was the pre-incarnate Son of God. It is he who occupies Jehovah's throne, who is too holy to behold and who is the centre of heaven's worship. He is no one less than the eternal God. No wonder one of heaven's rules is 'Let all the angels of God worship him'! (Hebrews 1:6).

Son of God

Side by side with this teaching that the Lord Jesus Christ is God in his own right runs the scriptural teaching that he is who he is because of the Father. We must now say a little about this doctrine of 'the eternal generation of the Son', lest it be misunderstood, and used as a reason for giving less glory to Christ than to the Father, or of thinking of him as a 'lesser' God.

Without any reference to his birth among us as a human, the Lord Jesus Christ is described as 'the only begotten of the Father' (John 1:14); 'the only begotten Son' (John 1:18; 3:16); and 'the only begotten Son of God' (John 3:18). The Son owes his generation to the Father, but the same cannot be said the other way round. On two other occasions the term 'first-born' is used—a term which simply underlines what he was before all creation (Colossians

1:15; Hebrews 1:6). The relationship between the Father and the Son is obviously unique. None the less, the Scripture is prepared to help our mortal minds to understand by speaking of it in terms of generation and birth. We have earlier read that the Son is the express image of God the Father and the shining forth of his glory (Hebrews 1:3). We are clearly meant to understand that it would be impossible for him to be what he is without God the Father. But God the Father is never said to be the express image of God the Son.

The changeless godhead

We are not suggesting that the Father *created* the Son. The Athanasian Creed is right to declare that 'The Son is from the Father alone, neither made, nor created, but begotten.' We have seen that the Lord Jesus Christ is not a creature. He is God as the Father is God. Both are God; both are God equally; both are God eternally, and both are God in the same sense. Nor are we saying that God the Father chose to do something, or that something which had not happened came to happen. We are talking about something which takes place naturally in the Godhead, and has always done so—something which is happening now, and has happened eternally. If this were not the case, there would be some change in the Godhead, and that is impossible. Besides, it would contradict the plain biblical teaching that Christ's 'goings forth have been from of old, from everlasting' (Micah 5:2; see Matthew 2:6; John 7:42).

God the Father does not *make* God the Son to be God. We repeat, he is God in his own right. And yet without God the Father, there would be no person in the Godhead who is God the Son. The Son is what he is because of God the Father. Within the Godhead there is something going on which is similar to thinking and speaking. The Son is the expression of the Father. We now begin to understand why he is said to be 'the Word', who is with God, and is God, from the beginning (John 1:1–2). This is what the Son is. He could not be this without God the Father.

The Father could not find expression without God the Son. This is the relationship which the first and second persons of the Trinity have to each other.

Scriptural truth

Scripture after Scripture speaks of the mysterious truth we are discussing. The Lord Jesus Christ is God in his own right; but think of the ways in which we have already seen him described. Not only is he the Word of God (John 1:1) and the exact representation of his nature (Hebrews 1:3), but he is also in the form of God (Philippians 2:6), 'the image of the invisible God' (Colossians 1:15; 2 Corinthians 4:4). The main point is constantly pressed upon us. The Son could not be what he is without God the Father. He is what he is *because* of God the Father.

It is important to emphasize that this relationship of the Son to the Father did not have a beginning. It has always been like this. We must never think that Jesus is only called 'the Son' since his birth as a man in this world. John 1:14–18 makes it clear that it was his taking flesh that enabled men to see the only begotten of the Father, but he was the only begotten *before* then. He was God's dear Son when he made the universe (Colossians 1:14–20). It was not a status which came later. In the same way both Romans 1:3 and Galatians 4:4 speak of him as being God's Son before they speak of his being born. He was the Son before he came in the likeness of sinful flesh (Romans 8:3). He was the Son before God sent him into the world (John 3:16; 1 John 4:9).

Hebrews 1:5–8 is a particularly important passage. As Son, the Lord Jesus Christ is declared to be God, and to reign upon an everlasting throne. It is he who as 'the first-begotten' (AV) is brought into the world. His sonship is eternal. This relationship with God the Father had no beginning. It is also unique and beyond our comprehension: 'No one knows the Son except the Father. Nor does anyone know the Father except the Son, and he to whom the Son wills to reveal him' (Matthew 11:27).

The divine Messiah

The purpose of this opening chapter has been to demonstrate the eternal deity of our Lord Jesus Christ. Our next chapter will examine his coming among us, and will show that his deity was even *clearer* after his incarnation than before. To prepare us for that, we need to close this chapter by showing that even before his coming into the world, it was made evident that the coming Messiah would be no one less than God. Let us look at a few selected examples.

Psalm 2 speaks of a king who is specifically said to be God's Son, and to whom universal power is promised over the whole earth and its inhabitants. Everyone is exhorted to submit to him and to trust him, lest they should experience his anger. Like all the passages cited in this section, the Jews understood this to be a reference to their coming Messiah, although they decidedly played down the references to his deity, which none the less remained too obvious to miss. In Acts 13:33 Paul declares that this psalm refers to the Lord Jesus Christ. The Messiah was spoken of in divine terms long before he ever appeared in the flesh. He was known to be the Son of God centuries before he assumed human nature.

Psalm 45 was also considered by the Jews to refer to the Messiah, and the fact is established by the writer to the Hebrews in Hebrews 1:8-9. Those verses make it quite clear that it is proper to call Jesus God, and to refer to his throne as eternal. They also show that 'the Son' is something that he *is*, intrinsically, and not something that he *became* at his incarnation.

That Psalm 110 also refers to the Messiah is proved beyond all doubt by the Lord Jesus Christ himself (Matthew 22:43-44), and by the writer to the Hebrews (Hebrews 5:6; 7:17). He is called David's Lord and the term used is *Adonai*, an ascription only ever used of the supreme God, the God of Israel. This God is invited to sit at the right hand of Jehovah until his enemies should be made his footstool. This is but one of many Old Testament references which unveil the stunning truth that there is one who is separate from God, who is none the less God himself!

The testimony of the prophets

Similar information is scattered throughout the prophets. Isaiah 9:6 speaks of the coming Messiah as '[the] Mighty God' (see Matthew 4:14–16). That is his identity *at* birth, and not an exalted title given to him later. Jeremiah sees him as 'the LORD [namely 'Jehovah'] our Righteousness' (Jeremiah 23:6). Zechariah has the holy audacity to present him as the man who is Jehovah's 'companion' or associate! (Zechariah 13:7; see Matthew 26:31). There was no mistaking whom the Jews were to expect. Their human Messiah would be possessed of deity. He would be one of the Godhead. He would be God himself!

It is hard to understand how the Jews failed to recognize Christ's true identity, when at last he came. The only explanation can be their unhealed spiritual blindness. The last prophet of their canon spoke of the one they awaited as 'the Lord, whom you seek' (Malachi 3:1). Once more the word used is *Adonai*. The temple, which was sacred to the worship of Jehovah, was called '*his* temple'. To remove the final vestiges of doubt it was declared that this coming Messiah would engage in the divine work of judgement (Malachi 3:2). It was obvious whom they were to expect!

They were also told that the coming of their divine Messiah need not take them by surprise. He would be preceded by a messenger, who would prepare the way for him. A few minutes after this prediction the prophetic voice fell silent, and generation after generation lived and died without hearing any man bring any further authoritative message from heaven.

The silence broken

It was four hundred years before the silence was broken. On Jordan's banks stood John the Baptist, claiming to be the forerunner of whom Malachi had spoken (Mark 1:2; John 1:23).

In dress, demeanour and message he was just like Elijah, and this made it even more apparent that he was the fulfilment of Malachi's predictions (Malachi 4:5–6; see Matthew 11:7–15). The advent of the promised messenger meant that the coming of 'the Lord', the promised Messiah, could not be far behind. The whole nation was stirred. For whom, precisely, was John preparing the way? Whom exactly had he come to herald? He would identify him soon, but who would it be?

The next day John saw Jesus coming towards him, and said, 'Behold! The Lamb of God who takes away the sin of the world! This is he of whom I said, "After me comes a man who is preferred before me, for he was before me." I did not know him; but that he should be revealed to Israel, therefore I came baptizing with water.'

And John bore witness, saying, 'I saw the Spirit descending from heaven like a dove, and he remained upon him. I did not know him, but he who sent me to baptize with water said to me, "Upon whom you see the Spirit descending, and remaining on him, this is he who baptizes with the Holy Spirit." And I have seen and testified that this is the Son of God' (John 1:29–34).

But what John pointed out to them they failed to see. The fault was not with John. His testimony to Christ was plain enough. The fault was with themselves. Pride, under its common guises of prejudice and unbelief, had blinded them to the obvious. If we do not accept the Bible's testimony to the identity of Christ, it will be for the same reason. Worshipping hearts have no trouble in recognizing him.

> Thou art the everlasting Word,
> The Father's only Son;
> God manifestly seen and heard,
> And Heaven's beloved One.
>
> In thee most perfectly expressed

The Father's glories shine;
Of the full Deity possessed,
Eternally Divine.

True image of the Infinite,
Whose essence is concealed;
Brightness of uncreated light;
The heart of God revealed.

But the high mysteries of Thy name
An angel's grasp transcend;
The Father only—glorious claim!
The Son can comprehend.

Throughout the universe of bliss,
The centre Thou, and sun;
The eternal theme of praise is this,
To Heaven's beloved One:

Worthy, O Lamb of God, art Thou
That every knee to Thee should bow.

Josiah Conder, 1789–1855.

Endnote

[1] I have already written a straightforward study of what the Bible teaches about the Trinity in *The Three are One* (paperback, Evangelical Press, 1979). This present book sometimes overlaps that one in its consideration of the deity of Christ. It is otherwise quite separate from it, and is its logical sequel.

2
God with us

We have seen that the Lord Jesus Christ was eternally God. The purpose of this chapter is to show that he did not become *less* than God by becoming a man. It is true that he became what he was not before—a theme that we will discuss in chapter 5. But he continued to be what he always was. His entrance into the world was as 'God with us' (Matthew 1:23). He was the one in whom dwelt 'all the fulness of the Godhead bodily' (Colossians 2:9).

Once more we are face to face with a great mystery. How the pre-existent Son of God could assume human nature, and take to himself human flesh and blood, is beyond our mortal understanding. We underline what we must never forget. We are able to state *what* the truth is, because the Scriptures reveal it. But we simply cannot comprehend *how* it can be so. How can the Infinite walk this finite world as a finite man? How can the Supernatural enter the historical life of this planet? '*Great* is the mystery of godliness ...' (1 Timothy 3:16).

Understood or not, it remains a fact that 'The Word *became* flesh', as we should correctly translate John 1:14. The wording of this verse is very careful. No hint is given that the Word ceased to be what he was previously. He was exactly the same after his incarnation as before. He did not change *into* flesh, and thus alter his essential nature. He was the infinite and unchangeable Son of

God, and this is what he remained. But by a process of addition he took to himself all that is comprehended by the word *flesh* (Greek: *sarx*), namely a complete human nature, consisting of body and soul. We will return to this point later. Our single aim at this moment is to keep stressing that while he was among us, the Lord Jesus Christ continued to be fully God.

Manifested in the flesh

The stunning mystery of the incarnation is that he who continued to be what he always was, was now 'manifested in the flesh' (1 Timothy 3:16). He came into the position where he could be heard, seen and handled. But this did not make him any less than the one who 'was from the beginning ... the Word of life'. The great difference was that 'the life was manifested ... manifested to us'. Which life? 'That eternal life which was with the Father' (see 1 John 1:1–2). Those who saw Christ 'beheld his glory, the glory as of the only begotten of the Father' (John 1:14). They saw no one less than the eternally generated Son of God! The incarnation made no difference whatever to his essential deity. Instead, for the first time, deity was unveiled before human eyes. 'No one has seen God at any time. The only begotten Son, who is in the bosom of the Father, he has declared him' (John 1:18).

To explain this truth to their children, some of the Puritans used to refer to the ancient Kings of Sparta. On several occasions in Spartan history several kings reigned at the same time, in joint authority with one another. From time to time a king was sent to a neighbouring state in the character of a Spartan ambassador. Did he, when sent in this way, cease to be a King of Sparta? His role of ambassador did not divest him of his royal dignity. So Christ, in becoming man, did not cease to be God. He continued to be the King of creation, as he always had been. His becoming the voluntary messenger and servant of his Father in no way altered this.

This truth can be realized with a powerful freshness if we

ponder Paul's words in Philippians 2:7. There, among other things, the apostle tells us that Christ 'took upon him the form of a servant' (AV). Every creature is, by the mere fact of its creation, the servant of its maker. It cannot take upon itself the form of a servant, because that is what it already is. But not so Christ, declares Paul. The form of a servant is something *he took upon himself*. Such language could not be used in the context of incarnation if the person concerned was anyone other than God himself.

His birth

The eternal Son of God was constituted one of the human race by means of a supernatural conception and a virgin birth. It was not a mere baby that was begotten. It was the eternal Son of God in respect of his human nature. In our previous chapter we surveyed a chain of Old Testament promises which insisted that a man was coming, who was in fact God! This event was the fulfilment of what God had said so often, and for so long.

But, as Matthew 1:22-23 reminds us, Christ's birth was also the fulfilment of a very specific prophecy made by Isaiah seven centuries earlier. In speaking to King Ahaz he had declared, 'Therefore the Lord himself will give you a sign: Behold, the virgin shall conceive and bear a Son, and shall call his name Immanuel ["God with us"]' (Isaiah 7:14).

Ahaz had been fearful that his kingdom of Judah would be wiped out by the combined might of Syria and Israel, and Isaiah's commission had been to assure the king that their plans would come to nothing. He had invited the king to ask for a sign from God that this would be so, but he had refused. It was therefore stated that, whether he asked or not, the Lord himself would give a sign. A virgin would bear a child who would be God!

It was made plain that the child would not be born at once. When he was a weaned child, and capable of distinguishing one kind of food from another, he would eat 'curds and honey' (7:15).

These commodities were normally freely available in Canaan, but never during time of war, on account of the pillaging of troops. It was therefore plain that the child would not be born during the present hostilities. Indeed, it is categorically stated that at the time of his weaning both Syria and Israel would have ceased to exist (7:16).

The promised sign was therefore evidently a future event. What then was the point of mentioning it to Ahaz? What comfort could it possibly have given him at the time when he thought his kingdom was about to be destroyed?

God was saying that Judah could never be wiped out, because he had a future purpose for it. Did not Judah belong to *him*? Was it not *Immanuel's land*? (8:8). How could Immanuel, 'God with us', be born there if Judah ceased to exist? The future coming of the virgin's son was sufficient guarantee that the nation of Judah would never be exterminated. If it was, the divine promise would have to be broken. That, by definition, is impossible. No, at last the nation would again include Galilee (9:1), and then would come the 'Child … born … Mighty God … upon the throne of David' (9:6–7).

Angelic visitation

Seven hundred years later two members of the tribe of Judah who lived in Galilee were each visited by an angel. It was Gabriel who brought the first message to Mary, a virgin girl of Nazareth:

> Then the angel said to her, 'Do not be afraid, Mary, for you have found favour with God. And behold, you will conceive in your womb and bring forth a Son, and shall call his name Jesus. He will be great, and will be called the Son of the Highest; and the Lord God will give him the throne of his father David. And he will reign over the house of Jacob for ever, and of his kingdom there will be no end.'
>
> Then Mary said to the angel, 'How can this be, since I do not know a man?' And the angel answered and said to her,

'The Holy Spirit will come upon you, and the power of the Highest will overshadow you; therefore, also, that Holy One who is to be born will be called the Son of God' (Luke 1:30–35).

Joseph was shocked to find his wife-to-be pregnant, not knowing that she was 'with child of the Holy Spirit' (Matthew 1:18). Although he and Mary were not man and wife in the full sense, their commitment to each other could not be broken without a divorce. Such were the customs of the time. Upright man that he was, and evidently in love with Mary, he determined to do this as quietly as possible.

But while he thought about these things, behold, an angel of the Lord appeared to him in a dream, saying, 'Joseph, son of David, do not be afraid to take to you Mary your wife, for that which is conceived in her is of the Holy Spirit. And she will bring forth a Son, and you shall call his name Jesus, for he will save his people from their sins.'

Now all this was done that it might be fulfilled which was spoken by the Lord through the prophet, saying: 'Behold, a virgin shall be with child, and bear a Son, and they shall call his name Immanuel, which is translated, "God with us"' (Matthew 1:20–23).

His self-consciousness

An awareness of his divine identity was something which Jesus carried with him throughout his life. He was conscious of his unique relationship with God, and consistently mindful that he was his eternal Son. What he had known eternally was in no way suspended by his becoming incarnate.

This is obvious even from his earliest recorded words, spoken when he was a boy of twelve. 'His mother said to him, "Son, why have you done this to us? Look, your *father* and I have sought you anxiously." And he said to them, "Why is it that you sought me? Did you not know that I must be about my *Father's business?*'" (Luke 2:48–49, emphasis mine). He at once offset the slightest suggestion that he had a human father, and insisted that it should be regarded as natural that he should be in his Father's house. This he spoke in the temple—the house of God!

When Jesus opened his mouth in public teaching, the same divine self-consciousness shone through. He spoke with a unique authority which staggered those who heard him (Matthew 7:28–29; John 7:32,45–46). His hearers were accustomed to the teaching of the Jewish scribes, who spent most of their time quoting learned writers. Jesus did not speak like them. But nor did he speak like the prophets, who had prefaced their messages with 'Thus says the Lord'. He spoke on his *own* authority, saying, 'I say to you' (Matthew 5:18,20,22 etc.). He spoke, self-consciously, as God.

Christ's identity

Christ's personal awareness of his identity is seen most clearly in John's Gospel. Scores of verses could be quoted, and we must be selective. But a good example is John 5:16–47, where Jesus speaks at length about his unique relationship with God the Father. The Greek of verse 18 shows that he called God 'his *own* Father'—in other words, God was Father to him in a way in which he was not to anybody else. This came across clearly to the Jews who were listening, and they were furious that he made himself equal with God in this way (vv. 17–18). It is striking that Jesus' consciousness of his eternal generation did not lessen his consciousness of being equal with God. Yet he went on to show that although he did the same works as the Father, he was unable to work independently of his Father (vv. 19–24). He could only judge because the Father had committed judgement to him (v. 22). But this did not mean that he was to be treated as inferior to the Father. By no means! Indeed, he was to be given the honour that was given to the Father! (v. 23). If the Son was not honoured in this way, then the Father did not receive the honour due to *him*. So he was aware of his sonship, and aware that his Father had sent him. Yet, incomprehensibly to our minds, he was aware of his equality and unity with the Father!

As the passage continues, Jesus claims that he has life in himself, as does the Father. Unlike us, he was not made alive by anyone. Even so, he goes on to say that he has life in himself, only because the Father gave him this quality! (v. 26). The divine prerogative of raising the dead also belongs to the Son of God (v. 25); and yet he can do nothing on his own initiative. All the power he exercises is because of his Father who has sent him into the world, and whose will he loves to obey (vv. 30,36). He comes exercising divine powers (v. 40), and as the subject of the Scriptures (vv. 39,46), and yet he does not come in his own name, but in his Father's (v. 43). The whole passage shows that Jesus knew himself to be God, in and of himself. He is God in his own right. But he also knew that he would be *nothing at all* if it were not for God the Father. He was not simply aware of a unique relationship with God, but was able to define precisely what that relationship was. Human lips spoke what no human has ever been able to comprehend. This in itself was yet one further demonstration that he who spoke was none other than God himself.

Similar passages are found in John chapters 8 and 10. John chapter 8 begins with the narrative of the woman taken in adultery. After Jesus had invited whoever was without sin to cast the first stone, her accusers left, one by one. Jesus remained, spoke as one who had the right to condemn her, but who would not, and commanded her not to sin again. The incident makes it evident that Christ's own consciousness was permeated with a sense of his own sinlessness and with the awareness that he had the divine right to condemn, to forgive and to give absolute moral commands.

The Son's relationship to the Father

The rest of the chapter is filled with references to his relationship with the Father. Jesus declared that he knew where he had come from and where he was going (v. 14). From where had he come? 'From above … I am not of this world' (v. 23). He had been sent into the world by his Father (vv. 16,18,26); 'for I proceeded forth and came from God; nor have I come of myself, but he sent me' (v. 42).

Where was he going? He was going where his hearers could not come; and this was obviously the same place from which he had come (vv. 21-24). It was no good the Jews asking where his Father was, for if they had known Christ, they would have known the Father (v. 19). Jesus was quite clear that to know him was to know *God*!

What was his relationship with the Father? He was never alone, because he had his constant company (v. 16). This was because he always did those things which pleased him (v. 29). The fellowship was thus never broken. The Father was a constant witness to him (v. 18). He honoured the Father (v. 49) and the Father honoured him (v. 54). He spoke only what he had heard from the Father, and had seen with him (vv. 26,38), and this, of course, meant that the words he spoke were the words of God (vv. 45-47). There was nothing that he did on his own initiative, but he acted and spoke only as he had been taught by the Father (v. 28). The relationship was unique, and he knew the Father as nobody else did (v. 55).

The Son was obviously distinct from the Father, but did this mean that he was less God than the Father was? Not at all! Verse 12 contains one of Jesus' many 'I AM' utterances, which were undoubted assumptions of deity. Two more claims to be 'I AM' are found in verses 24 and 28, though those who read too quickly to ponder each verse often fail to notice them. The chapter closes with the astonishing claim which we have considered earlier: 'Before Abraham was, I AM' (v. 58). This open claim to deity scandalized the Jews, who understood exactly what Jesus was saying, and were on the point of executing him for blasphemy.

Their reaction added further weight to the words which he had spoken only minutes before: 'Because I tell the truth, you do not believe me' (v. 45).

In his Father's name

In John 10:22–42 Jesus once more speaks of coming in his Father's name, and now also of the fact that those he has come to save are his only because the Father gave them to him (vv. 25–29). He is in the world only because the Father sent him (v. 36). This is the language of subordination. It reveals that the Son serves the Father. And yet in the same passage Christ's claims to deity are so obvious that the Jews once more thought of killing him (v. 31). They accused him of claiming to be God (v. 33), and they were not mistaken. That is exactly what Jesus *was* claiming! He claimed that he could do what God alone can do—that is, give eternal life (v. 28). He claimed that he, like the Father, could not have those whom he had saved snatched from his grasp (vv. 28–29). He claimed to be the Son of God, who was none the less one with the Father (vv. 36,30). He did not mean that he was one with his Father in the sense that a human son is. Such a person owes all that he is to his father; and so does the Son of God. Such a person is a separate person from his father; and so is the Son of God—in the sense that we use the word 'person' when talking of the Trinity. But such a person could never say, 'The Father is *in* me, and I *in* him' (v. 38; see John 14:10–11). The Son is separate from the Father. The Son is subordinate to the Father, and sent into the world by him. Yet the Son is one with the Father, and is God, as he is. Not only so, but each one is *in* the other. *This* is the mystery of the eternal generation of the Son. It is the mystery of the 'Son of God, begotten of his Father before all worlds, God of God, Light of Light, very God of very God, begotten, not made, being of one substance with the Father' (*Nicene Creed*). This was the mystery of which Jesus was continually conscious.

We do not find Jesus in any situation where he is without this divine self-awareness. In prayer we find him revelling in the fact that 'All things have been delivered to me by my Father, and no one knows the Son except the Father. Nor does anyone know the Father except the Son, and he to whom the Son wills to reveal him' (Matthew 11:27). In public teaching he makes the point that to speak a word against him is 'sin and blasphemy', which could only be true if he were possessed of deity (Matthew 12:31–32). This last remark is particularly powerful because it was indirect. It was almost an aside, or parenthesis, when our Lord was concentrating on another subject. It reveals just how deep-rooted the consciousness of his own identity really was.

The Messiah

We can now well understand why ascriptions of deity brought the Lord Jesus Christ such satisfaction and joy. They were true, and he knew it. He blesses Peter for his confession, 'You are the Christ, the Son of the living God' (Matthew 16:16), and welcomes his statement: 'You have the words of eternal life. Also we have come to believe and know that you are the Christ, the Son of the living God' (John 6:68–69). Knowing perfectly well that the Old Testament Scriptures promised a divine Messiah (or 'Christ', as it is in Greek), he did not hesitate to receive such an ascription, or even actually to claim such Messiahship for himself (John 4:25–26).

The title 'Son of God' which Peter used was well understood by the Jews to be a title for one who was fully God. This can be illustrated by what took place when Jesus stood trial the night before his crucifixion. The high priest put him on oath and asked him, 'I adjure you by the living God that you tell us if you are the Christ, the Son of God' (Matthew 26:63). Jesus admitted this to be true. Matthew tells us what followed: 'Then the high priest tore his clothes, saying, "He has spoken blasphemy! What further need do we have of witnesses? Look, now you have heard his blasphemy!"' (Matthew 26:65). He was perfectly convinced that Jesus had spoken blasphemy, because he understood perfectly that the title 'Son of God' is a divine title. Of course, it was not blasphemy but the truth—a truth which the high priest and the Jewish council refused to believe.

His heralds

But not every voice in the ancient world spoke in contradiction of the self-consciousness of Christ. We have mentioned what Peter said, speaking as he did for all the disciples. But there were other voices too—heavenly, earthly and even demonic which spoke the truth about Christ's identity.

Angelic testimony

The first of these was that of the angel who announced Messiah's birth to the astonished shepherds near Bethlehem. 'Behold,' he said, 'I bring you good tidings of great joy which will be to all people. For there is born to you this day in the city of David a Saviour, who is *Christ the Lord*' (Luke 2:10-11, emphasis mine). Right from the beginning there was to be no doubt about the precise identity of the one who entered the world by Mary's womb.

We have already mentioned that Jesus did not commence his public ministry until the way had been prepared for him by John the Baptist. But over thirty years earlier, the angel Gabriel had announced not only the ministry of the unborn John, but also of the one whom he was to precede.

> He will be great in the sight of the Lord, and shall drink neither wine nor strong drink. He will also be filled with the Holy Spirit, even from his mother's womb. And he will turn many of the children of Israel to *the Lord their God*. He will also go *before him* in the spirit and power of Elijah, 'to turn the hearts of the fathers to the children', and the disobedient to the wisdom of the just, to make ready a people prepared for *the Lord* (Luke 1:15-17, emphasis mine).

When John was born, his father Zacharias was filled with the Holy Spirit, and announced, 'You, child, will be called the prophet of *the Highest*; for you will go *before the face of the Lord* to prepare *his* ways, to give knowledge of salvation to his people by the remission of their sins' (Luke 1:76–77, emphasis mine). There was no possibility of misunderstanding. The person whom John was to herald was to be none other than God!

John the Baptist's testimony

What Gabriel and Zacharias had said was also clear to John himself. He saw his role in the same terms. He was not only the messenger foretold by Malachi, but was also the fulfilment of the prophecy of Isaiah 40:3: 'The voice of one crying in the wilderness: "Prepare the way of the Lord; make straight in the desert a highway for our God"' (see John 1:22–23). In the East, a forerunner often went ahead of a very important person. It was his job to smooth the road, so that the dignitary who was following did not have too bumpy a ride. John the Baptist was clear that the one who was following him was none other than Jehovah himself!

Heavenly testimony

When Jesus came to Jordan, John, as we have seen, positively identified him as the one of whom he had been speaking (John 1:29–30). Jesus is Jehovah! Jesus is God! Yet John's titles for the promised one were 'Lamb of God' and 'Son of God' (John 1:29,34). What all the Jews were clear about, John was clear about too. The Son of God is God. But the Son is not the Father, for as John baptized Jesus, a voice sounded from heaven, declaring, 'You are my beloved Son; in you I am well pleased' (Luke 3:22).

There was another occasion when the voice from heaven gave unambiguous testimony to the identity of Christ. But on this occasion there was more than a voice. The body of Jesus shone with celestial brightness. The glory of his Godhead was seen. His face was altered, and his garments became white and glistening. The description makes it clear that the illumination was not just external, as from a spotlight. The change came from within. The

Greek words used by the Gospel authors show that his clothes gave off dazzling flashes of light. It was as Peter, James and John witnessed this astonishing transfiguration that a heavenly voice declared, 'This is my beloved Son, in whom I am well pleased' (Matthew 17:5).

Peter wanted the scene to go on for ever, but this was not allowed him. But neither he nor the others could ever wipe out the memory of it from their minds. Half a century later John still recalled it with awe, and wrote, 'We beheld his glory, the glory as of the only begotten of the Father' (John 1:14). The indelible impression made on Peter is recorded in his words, preserved for us in his second letter: 'We ... were eyewitnesses of his majesty. For he received from God the Father honour and glory when such a voice came to him from the Excellent Glory: "This is my beloved Son, in whom I am well pleased." And we heard this voice which came from heaven when we were with him on the holy mountain' (2 Peter 1:16–18).

There was normally nothing about the physical appearance of Christ to reveal his divine identity. The transfiguration was special, and took place only once. It was an opportunity for three witnesses to see what was normally veiled. But the fact that it was veiled did not alter the truth of it. Jesus of Nazareth was incarnate Deity!

Demonic testimony

But what was normally hidden from human eyes was not hidden from the spirit world. During his public ministry, our Lord Jesus Christ met many demon-possessed men and women. But he did not come to them as a mere exorcist, as was clear to see. Jewish exorcists of the period cast out demons only after a lengthy and complicated ritual. Jesus cast them out with a word, and at once attracted universal astonishment (Mark 1:27).

As the demons came out, they heralded the identity of the one who had such unquestionable power over them. In Capernaum's synagogue they cried, 'What have we to do with you, Jesus of Nazareth? Did you come to destroy us? I know who you are—the Holy One of God!' (Mark 1:24). Extraordinarily similar is the declaration which came from the lips of the Gadarene demoniacs, 'What have we to do with you, Jesus, you Son of God? Have you come here to torment us before the time?' (Matthew 8:29). But Jesus was not willing to have his glory heralded to an unbelieving world by the wicked powers which controlled it, and frequently stopped such testimonies from proceeding any further. People must come to see who he is as the result of a spiritual discernment which is always married to a repentant spirit, and not because of the shouts of terrified spirits who fear that the day of their final damnation has arrived.

The apostle Paul's testimony

The joyous proclamation of the angels, the plain preaching of the Baptist, the awesome dogmatism of the heavenly voice and the terrified and reluctant admission of damned spirits was also the message of the apostles after the resurrection and ascension of the Lord. Less than the least of the apostles, but the one who laboured more fruitfully than them all, was the apostle Paul. The first truth about Jesus that he proclaimed after his conversion was 'that he is the Son of God', 'that this Jesus is the Christ' (Acts 9:20,22). He had no doubt that he who was so recently crucified at Jerusalem was the promised Messiah and possessed of a divine identity.

The man who had been born, had lived, died and risen again, was God's 'Son Jesus Christ our Lord, who was born of the seed of David according to the flesh, and declared to be the Son of God with power, according to the Spirit of holiness, by the resurrection from the dead, through whom we have received grace and apostleship' (Romans 1:3–5).

The incarnation had been the process of 'God … sending his own Son in the likeness of sinful flesh' (Romans 8:3). Yes! 'When the fulness of the time had come, God sent forth his Son, born of a woman, born under the law, to redeem those who were under the law, that we might receive the adoption as sons' (Galatians 4:4).

It never occurred to the apostles that the incarnation had in any way robbed the Son of God of his eternal and essential deity, or had in any way diminished it. They knew nothing of such a low view of Christ. The message which they heralded to the world was the lofty teaching of Hebrews 1:1-3, to which we have referred already. God himself has come among us, and returned as a man to the majesty from which he came: 'God, who at various time and in different ways spoke in times past to the fathers by the prophets, has in these last days spoken to us by his Son, whom he has appointed heir of all things, through whom also he made the worlds; who being the brightness of his glory and the express image of his person, and upholding all things by the word of his power, when he had by himself purged our sins, sat down at the right hand of the Majesty on high.'

His life

With the exception of Paul, all the apostles had witnessed the earthly life and ministry of the Lord Jesus Christ. If they ever doubted his deity, they had only to cast their minds back to what they had seen of him, to be convinced all over again.

For instance, had not the Lord Jesus Christ, even as a man, manifested attributes which belong to God alone? For example, he was clearly omniscient. On several occasions he had read people's hearts (Matthew 9:4; Luke 6:8; John 1:47; 2:24-25; 4:17-19). From the beginning he knew exactly who would betray him (John 6:70-71; 13:10-11). He predicted the details of his own death and resurrection (Matthew 16:21) and Peter's denial and restoration (Luke 22:31-34). And had not the thoughts of his disciples been plain to him, even when he was physically distant from them? (Mark 9:33-37; Luke 9:47). And the expressed doubts of Thomas, even when he was physically *absent*? (John 20:24-29).

Omnipresence is another divine attribute. Although it was manifestly obvious that Jesus was physically present in only one place at a time, on several occasions his language suggested more than that. Talking one night with Nicodemus, he claimed not only to be 'he who came down from heaven', but also 'the Son of Man who is *in* heaven' (John 3:13, emphasis mine). His evident humanity did not prevent him from continuing to operate in that spiritual dimension which had always been his, and to exercise his divine prerogatives there. No less surprising was his promise, even while physically on earth, to be present wherever two or three gathered in his name (Matthew 18:20). And it was from physical lips that the apostles heard his promise: 'And lo, I am with you always, even to the end of the age' (Matthew 28:20). Who but God himself could have said all these things, and made such a promise?

We have already commented on Jesus' divine authority in teaching. With the same authority he spoke to the winds and waves, and they obeyed him (Mark 4:41). He spoke to the blind, and they could see; to the deaf, and they could hear (Matthew 9:27–33; Mark 7:34–35). At his word the lame walked, the diseased were healed and even the dead were raised! (John 5:8–9; Luke 17:11–19; Mark 5:41–42; Luke 7:14–15; John 11:43–44). Most Godlike of all, he forgave sins (Mark 2:7–10; John 8:11).

Just as Jesus said they should, these words and works proved his identity (John 5:17,21,36). Those who heard his words, and witnessed his miracles, sensed themselves to be in the presence of God (Luke 5:25–26; 7:16; 9:43). In these references the emotion expressed was that of amazement and wonderment. But it was not always so. When Peter witnessed one of the early miracles, the sense that he was in God's presence was so strong that 'he fell down at Jesus' knees, saying, "Depart from me, for I am a sinful man, O Lord!"' (Luke 5:8). On another occasion his disciples 'came and worshipped him, saying, "Truly you are the Son of God"' (Matthew 14:33).

And the man Christ Jesus did not turn such worship away. Far from it, for he taught that 'All should honour the Son just as they honour the Father. He who does not honour the Son does not honour the Father who sent him' (John 5:23).

His death and resurrection

Just as Christ's life stressed his deity, so did the events of Calvary and the forty days between his resurrection and his triumphant return to heaven.

Those who witnessed the crucifixion of our Lord Jesus Christ saw something that no one had ever seen before. The final act of a crucified man is to lift up his head. In a last attempt at self-preservation, he tries to get as much air as possible into his lungs. But Jesus' death was different. He bowed 'his head, [and] … gave up his spirit' (John 19:30).

Our Lord voluntarily bowed his head and died. It was he who decided the precise moment at which his death would take place. When it came, he submissively gave up his life to his Father, confidently uttering the words: 'Father, "into your hands I commend my spirit"' (Luke 23:46). He bowed his head and his body immediately hung limp in death, without the final panic of other men who die fighting the inevitable.

The word 'commend' can accurately be translated 'lay down'. Our Lord's dismissing of his own spirit was the open demonstration of words which he had earlier spoken before the Jews: 'I lay down my life that I may take it again. No one takes it from me, but I lay it down of myself. I have power to lay it down, and I have power to take it again. This command I have received from my Father' (John 10:17–18).

No ordinary death

Christ's death displayed that it was no ordinary man who was on the cross. While it is true that he had his life taken from him, it is also true that it only took place with his permission. Before allowing his enemies to arrest him, he proved his divine power by repeating his divine name of 'I am', and causing them to fall backwards to the ground (John 18:1-11). But having permitted himself to be arrested, he steadfastly refused to use his almighty power to deliver himself from death, although he could have done so at any time. He chose to die the death of the cross.

The New Testament is in no doubt about the identity of the person who hung on Golgotha's cross. A wicked world 'crucified the Lord of glory' (1 Corinthians 2:8). The one who purchased his church 'with his own blood' was God! (Acts 20:28). '*God* was in Christ reconciling the world to himself' (2 Corinthians 5:19, emphasis mine). Deity is ascribed to Jesus Christ, even at the moment of his dying. It was not God the Father who died, nor was it God the Holy Spirit. But the victim was God none the less—God the Son (Hebrews 1:1-3). His death in no way robbed him of this identity, for 'though he was a Son, yet he learned obedience by the things which he suffered' (Hebrews 5:8). The essence of personal faith is to look at Calvary, and to declare that 'The Son of God … loved me and gave himself for me' (Galatians 2:20).

Resurrection attestation

But our Lord's resurrection provided an even greater demonstration of his deity. He had predicted it, and if it had not taken place, he would have been for ever discredited as Redeemer and Son of God. But it did take place! Attempts to explain it away, or to deny its factuality, have their root in disbelief of the supernatural, and not in any objective examination of the evidence, which is totally convincing. The resurrection of Christ stands on the pages of history as a well-attested and unassailed fact. God's raising of Christ from the dead owned and declared him to be his Son. The act set God's imprimatur upon our Lord's deity (Romans 1:4). During his life our Lord had claimed to be the Son of God, but his enemies had constantly rejected the claim. It was his repeating of this claim under oath that convinced the Jews that he was guilty of blasphemy, and moved them to condemn him to die (Matthew 26:63-66). When he was crucified they obtained from Pontius Pilate permission to seal the entrance to his tomb and to have it guarded, for they remembered that he had said, when alive, 'After three days I will rise' (Matthew 27:62-66). These words had obviously made a deep impression on their minds and induced them to set a guard of soldiers on his tomb. They certainly wanted to justify their own conduct in putting him to death as a deceiver, and may perhaps have intended to examine his body after the third day, and to have used the fact of its continuance in the grave as a means of scorning him further, and of deriding the grief-stricken men and women who had followed him.

Christ's enemies triumphed in his death, but their rejoicing was short. In spite of all opposition, God raised his Son from the dead. His resurrection was the powerful attestation of heaven that he really was who he said he was, and not a deceiver. His claims were thoroughly endorsed and proved to be true. Never again is there any need to doubt his deity. His sonship was the cause of his resurrection, and the resurrection the supreme evidence of that sonship.

Appearance to disciples

On the day that our Lord rose from the dead, he presented himself alive to his frightened disciples, who were met together behind locked doors. His death had shaken their faith in him, but the sight of him quickly restored it. However, one of their number, Thomas, was absent, and simply would not believe the others when they told him that they had seen the Lord. His retort was 'Unless I see in his hands the print of the nails, and put my finger into the print of the nails, and put my hand into his side, I will not believe' (John 20:25). John tells us about the events which followed: 'After eight days his disciples were again inside, and Thomas with them. Jesus came, the doors being shut, and stood in the midst, and said, "Peace to you!" Then he said to Thomas,

"Reach your finger here, and look at my hands; and reach your hand here, and put it into my side. Do not be unbelieving, but believing." And Thomas answered and said to him, "My Lord and my God!"' (John 20:26-28).

Jesus did not reject this astonishing confession from Thomas' lips. He did not say that his worship was blasphemous, and that God alone should be worshipped. He accepted it totally. Indeed, he replied, 'Thomas, because you have seen me, you have believed. Blessed are those who have not seen and yet have believed' (John 20:29). He made it clear that to believe in his deity is to be a believer. 'My Lord and my God' remains the adoring confession of true believers today. He is the object of their faith. It is by believing on him that they are saved (Acts 16:31). They know him as 'our great God and Saviour Jesus Christ' (Titus 2:13).

Ascension to glory

But such appearances of our Lord Jesus Christ to his disciples were not to go on for ever. The New Testament records what occurred forty days after his resurrection: 'He led them out as far as Bethany, and he lifted up his hands and blessed them. Now it came to pass, while he blessed them, that he was parted from them and carried up into heaven.' 'While they watched, he was taken up, and a cloud received him out of their sight ...' 'Received up into heaven, and sat down at the right hand of God' (Luke 24:50-51; Acts 1:9; Mark 16:19).

This astonishing event was the fulfilment of several earlier predictions. Our Lord himself had said, 'What then if you should see the Son of Man ascend where he was before?' and, 'I go to him who sent me' (John 6:62; 7:33). A thousand years earlier the psalmist had written of the Messiah, 'You have ascended on high ... you have received gifts among men' (Psalm 68:18; see Ephesians 4:8).

The post-resurrection appearances of Christ were intended to convince his disciples that he had conquered death, and to endorse his claim to deity. His ascension was intended to show them that they should not expect any further such appearances. How could his resurrection body be permanently at home on earth? He must depart, but by glorification, and not by dying again. The spectacular method of his departure was entirely fitting, in the light of his miraculous coming to the world of men and the miracles which he had performed since. Besides, the gift of his Holy Spirit to his church was dependent on his glorification (John 7:37–39).

Christ's ascension also gave his people the final assurance that the work he had come to do had been completed to the entire satisfaction of his Father. He was exalted to the Father's right hand, and took his seat there. The picture is of Christ reigning and exercising divine omnipotence. It speaks of his absolute sovereignty over the whole universe. And he is there because he has a right to be there. Who can now doubt that he who came among us is other than God himself? Who but God can sit on God's throne and exercise God's powers? The wonder is that the God who sits there does so as a man!

From the slopes of Bethany Christ ascended into heaven. As he entered through its portals he was greeted both by angelic spirits and 'the spirits of just men made perfect' (Hebrews 12:23):

> Ye gates, lift up your heads on high;
> Ye doors that last for aye,
> Be lifted up, that so the King
> Of glory enter may.
>
> But who of glory is the King?
> The mighty Lord is this;
> Ev'n that same Lord, that great in might
> And strong in battle is.
>
> Ye gates, lift up your heads; ye doors,
> Doors that do last for aye,

Be lifted up, that so the King
Of glory enter may.

But who is he that is the King
Of glory? Who is this?
The LORD of hosts, and none but he,
The King of glory is.

Psalm 24:7–10,
The Psalms in metre.

3

God—now and always

Just as our Lord did not cease to be God when he became man, so he did not cease to be God when he returned to heaven, even though he returned there with a human nature which he did not have until he came to earth. He is God now. And he always will be. This is the theme of our present chapter.

This doctrine is found in every single book of the New Testament, and taught repeatedly—either by direct assertion, or by necessary implication. Every impartial reader can see this for himself. The mass of the testimony is so great, and so intimately woven into the very fabric of the New Testament, that we do not need now to do anything more than to present a general sample of the evidence. He is God eternally: he was God while among us, and he is God now, and always. Indeed, how could anyone who had ever been God cease to be so? The idea is preposterous. One who is God is, by definition, God for ever. But the New Testament is eager to present a truth which cannot be missed. It does not leave us simply to think things through, and to come to the obvious conclusion. It states the truth clearly.

Two key paragraphs

In considering this theme, a good starting-point is a paragraph of the New Testament to which we have already referred several times. This is Hebrews 1:1–3. Why not open your Bible again at those magnificent words, and ponder them afresh?

Having told us that God's speaking to his world has reached its climax and its conclusion in his Son, the apostle proceeds to tell us seven marvellous truths about him. Christ is the mediatorial heir of the universe. It was by him that God made the worlds. He is the effulgence of his glory—the one who shines with God's glory, not by way of reflection, but intrinsically. He is the impress of God's substance and perfectly reveals him. By his word, he holds everything together. This is the one who by himself purged our sins and is now seated at the right hand of the Majesty on high.

In these verses the apostle tells us who and what Christ is, and what he has done. On God's throne, as a man, now sits one who still is the effulgence of God's glory and the impress of his substance. The humiliation of his incarnation and of his atoning work has not hindered his glorious exaltation to the place from which he came. But nor has it brought about any essential change in him. Christ remains what he is. What he was when he made the worlds, this he remains. And as we ponder the expressions used of him, we know full well that they could not be used of any other than of God himself. He who is now and for ever a man is still God.

Ephesians 4

Another important paragraph is Ephesians 4:7–8. Here Paul is making the point that the ascended Christ has given different gifts to each believer in the church. In support of this assertion he quotes Psalm 68:18. Paul could not possibly have done this if he had not been sure that that verse was about the Lord Jesus Christ.

A careful examination of Psalm 68:18 reveals that it is celebrating the arrival of the ark of the Lord in Jerusalem. Jerusalem has a unique dignity on earth, not because its Mount Zion is higher than other hills, but because of its spiritual elevation as the chosen dwelling-place of God. The verse quoted shows that after the conquest of what had been an enemy stronghold, Jehovah himself 'ascends' Mount Zion, to share the spoils of victory with his people. Paul, however, sees that these words have a still higher fulfilment in Christ's ascension. He has been exalted to the seat of universal sovereignty in heaven, from where he distributes gifts to his church. Paul is not content with anything less than such exalted language as he thinks of Christ in heaven. The thought simply does not cross his mind that Christ, a man in heaven, is less than God. A psalm exclusively about God, he ascribes to Christ. To think of the ascended Christ in terms of deity is, to him, as natural as breathing.

The two paragraphs we have referred to are typical of dozens of others in the New Testament. Christ is God *now and always*. But to show this as clearly as possible, let us follow four lines of thought on this subject which writers have used for centuries. They are exactly similar to the lines of thought which established that Christ is God eternally, but they are no less convincing because of that. Not just when referring to his eternal deity, not just when referring to the years when he was on earth, but when referring to him now, the New Testament calls Jesus God, ascribes to him the attributes of God, reveals that he does the works of God and teaches that he is to receive the honour and worship which are due to God alone. Once more let us follow such lines of thought one by one.

Names and titles

In the previous section we referred to Hebrews 1:1-3. That passage ended with a reference to Christ's ascension and present position. If we were to continue reading that chapter, we would discover that the writer proceeds directly to the point where the words of Psalm 45:6-7 are ascribed to Christ: 'Your throne, O God, is for ever and ever' (Hebrews 1:8). Jesus Christ, in the position in which he is now, is called God.

It is the eternal Christ, now ascended, whom Paul calls 'the eternally blessed God' (Romans 9:5); 'the King eternal, immortal, invisible … God who alone is wise' (1 Timothy 1:17); 'our great God and Saviour' (Titus 2:13) and he is the one of whom it can still be said, 'In him dwells all the fulness of the Godhead bodily' (Colossians 2:9).

To Peter, writing after his ascension, he is 'our God and Saviour'. This is how the Greek of 2 Peter 1:1 reads, and how it is translated by the New King James Version. To Jude, he is 'God our Saviour, who alone is wise' (Jude 24–25); and to John, 'the true God and eternal life' (1 John 5:20). We should note that it is not just others who made these stupendous claims for the ascended Lord. He made them himself. After his ascension, he revealed himself to John, exiled on the isle of Patmos, announcing himself in the following way: '"I am the Alpha and the Omega …" says the Lord, "who is and who was and who is to come, the Almighty"' (Revelation 1:8).

In addition to these plain statements, the divine title of 'Lord', which we examined earlier, continues to be used of the Lord Jesus Christ after his ascension. It is with an assertion of the lordship of Christ that the Christian church, in the full New Testament sense, is born: 'For David did not ascend into the heavens, but he says himself: "The Lord said to my Lord, 'Sit at my right hand, till I make your enemies your footstool.' Therefore let all the house of Israel know assuredly that God has made this Jesus, whom you crucified, both Lord and Christ" ' (Acts 2:34–36).

Christ's lordship

A belief in the lordship of Christ is so fundamental to the New Testament's understanding of his identity that it is plainly taught there that nobody can be considered to be a Christian who does not make this confession (1 Corinthians 12:3). We have already proved on pages 25–26 that this was a divine title. But this is further confirmed by Paul's words in 1 Corinthians 8:4b-6: 'We know that an idol is nothing in the world, and that there is no other God but one. For even if there are so-called gods, whether in heaven or on earth (as there are many gods and many lords), yet for us there is only one God, the Father, of whom are all things, and we for him; and one Lord Jesus Christ, through whom are all things, and through whom we live.' Paul's point here is not always easily followed. He is saying that although Christians know that there is but one God and Lord, pagan worshippers imagine their various deities to be real. This error needs to be opposed. There are not 'Gods a-plenty and Lords a-plenty' (B. B. Warfield), but one God the Father and one Lord Jesus Christ. Paul's language does not permit us to consider that he looks on these two as separate gods. There is but one God only. Deity is as much the possession of the Lord Jesus Christ as it is of the Father.

The same point comes across clearly in Romans 10:11–15. Paul has been explaining that it is only by faith in Christ that a person receives salvation, whether he be a Jew or a Gentile. In this context he writes, 'For "whoever calls upon the name of the LORD shall be saved"' (v. 13). 'The LORD' of whom he is writing is clearly Jesus Christ. Equally clearly, this verse is a citation of Joel 2:32, where the word translated 'LORD' in our Bibles is the Hebrew word 'Jehovah'. Paul is quite adamant that to call on Jehovah and to call on Christ is one and the same thing. There is no question in his mind. The title 'LORD' is a divine title which may properly be ascribed to Christ. It is hard to see how anyone could entertain any doubts on this point. But if such doubts persist, they must surely be dispelled by verse 15, where Paul clearly identifies the preaching of the gospel of Christ with, the message referred to in Isaiah 52:7: 'Your God reigns!'

In the same way the divine title 'Son of God' (see page 28) continues to be used of Christ after his ascension. As we have seen, this way of stating the deity of Christ was the first message that the apostle preached after his conversion (Acts 9:20), and was one of his favourite ways of referring to his Saviour for ever afterwards (for example, Galatians 2:20). The title is used by the writer to the Hebrews, when he is encouraging his readers to avail themselves of Christ's present high-priestly ministry (Hebrews 4:14–16). John also repeatedly uses the title when he is talking of a Christian's present experience of Christ (1 John 5:1–13). Whatever doubts may be nursed about the person of the Lord Jesus Christ today, the testimony of the New Testament is unambiguous. He was God while he was among us. He is God now!

Attributes

Not only is Jesus called God after his ascension, but the New Testament teaches that the characteristics which belong to God may continue to be ascribed to him.

Omnipresent

So far as space is concerned, God is everywhere (1 Kings 8:27; Psalm 139:7–10), but as we go into all the world to spread the gospel we are heartened to hear Christ's 'Lo, I am with you always' (Matthew 28:20). His presence everywhere is also displayed by his continuing promise to be wherever two or three gather in his name (Matthew 18:20). Wherever may be the person who loves Christ and keeps his words, he will know Christ's presence with him (John 14:23). Every Christian, wherever he is in the world, may know Christ in his heart (Ephesians 3:17). We shall see later that Christ's human nature cannot be everywhere, but this does not stop the attribute of omnipresence being attributed to him.

Eternal

So far as time is concerned, God is eternal (Isaiah 40:28; Habakkuk 1:12). In Isaiah 44:6 we read Jehovah asserting this of himself, saying, 'I am the first and I am the last.' Yet in Revelation Jesus says, 'I am the Alpha and the Omega, the beginning and the end, the first and the last' (Revelation 22:13, see also 1:11). Jehovah is eternal; Jesus is eternal. Clearly Jesus is Jehovah; he is God.

In Revelation 11:17 we read that those who surround God's throne say, 'We give you thanks, O Lord God Almighty, the One who is and who was and who is to come.' But in chapter 1:8, where the Lord Jesus Christ is speaking of himself, the words are almost identical. The ascended Christ is God!

Immutable

In this God there is no change. There never has been, and there never will be, for he is always the same (Malachi 3:6; James 1:17). But what is true of God alone is true of Jesus Christ ... the same yesterday, today, and for ever' (Hebrews 13:8). As he was before the universe was created, so is he now, and so will he be after it has vanished, for 'You, LORD, in the beginning laid the foundation of the earth, and the heavens are the work of your hands; they will perish, but you remain; and they will all grow old like a garment; like a cloak you will fold them up, and they will be changed. But you are the same, and your years will not fail' (Hebrews 1:10-12).

Omniscient

So far as knowledge is concerned, God knows everything (Psalm 139:2-5; 1 John 3:20). But no secrets are hidden from Christ. This note is struck seven times when, as the ascended Lord, he sends letters to his churches. After announcing his titles, each letter announces the solemn truth, 'I know your works' (Revelation 2:2,9,13,19; 3:1,8,15). Who else could say this but one who is God himself?

Omnipotent

So far as power is concerned, God does whatever he chooses (Psalm 135:6; Daniel 4:35). So does Jesus Christ. He is 'the Almighty' (Revelation 1:8). The whole universe is held together by his word (Hebrews 1:3). Without him, it would cease to exist

(Colossians 1:17). No wonder he is called 'King of kings and Lord of lords'! (Revelation 19:16; 1 Timothy 6:13-16). It was because of Christ's unfrustratable power that Paul was confident that he would personally arrive at last in heaven (2 Timothy 4:18). Yes, Jesus Christ is the one 'able even to subdue all things to himself (Philippians 3:21). And just as in Isaiah 45:23 Jehovah pledges, 'That to me every knee shall bow, every tongue shall take an oath,' so the New Testament pledges that God will cause 'that at the name of Jesus every knee should bow … and that every tongue should confess that Jesus Christ is Lord' (Philippians 2:10-11).

Holy and wise

Is God holy? Yet Peter, knowing this full well, is happy to refer Psalm 16 to Christ, and to call him the 'Holy One' (Acts 2:27). Can we say of God, 'Blessed be the name of God for ever and ever, for wisdom and might are his'? (Daniel 2:20). But it is right for us to call Jesus 'God our Saviour, who alone is wise' (Jude 24-25), 'God who alone is wise' (1 Timothy 1:17), 'in whom are hidden all the treasures of wisdom and knowledge' (Colossians 2:3). Again and again we see it: what is true of God alone is true of Jesus—now! What can be said of Jehovah alone is said of him. The conviction is borne in on us time and time again: Jesus is Jehovah! Jesus is God!

Divine works

During his time on earth, Jesus claimed that everything everywhere had been put into his hands by his Father (Luke 10:22; John 3:35). He could not have meant that this was true only for the few years that he walked the earth, because the New Testament insists that it is true of him now. Indeed, Christ's parting words were given to remind us that there is nowhere he does not rule (Matthew 28:18). All things are under his feet (Ephesians 1:22). Nothing happens anywhere unless it is Christ's will (Ephesians 1:11). All these things are divine works and prerogatives, and yet they are done by Christ!

'Who can forgive sins but God only?' But Paul wrote to the Colossians, 'As Christ forgave you, so you also must do' (Colossians 3:13). The Colossians had not become Christians until long after our Lord had gone back to heaven. They had never seen him or met him in the flesh. But what God alone can do, the ascended Christ had done for them!

Who but God can give eternal life? But Jesus made it plain that all who have eternal life have had it given to them by him (John 10:28). It is by his power that men and women become spiritually alive (John 5:21,25-27). No genuine spiritual experience can take place in a person's life without Jesus Christ being the author of it. He is the one who sends the Holy Spirit (John 16:7; Acts 2:32-33); and it is by him alone that the members of the Christian church are made holy (Ephesians 5:25-26).

But it is not only to spiritual life that Jesus raises people. It was in the context of physical death that he said, 'I am the resurrection and the life. He who believes in me, though he may die, he shall live. And whoever lives and believes in me shall never die' (John 11:25-26). But do we honestly believe that anyone less than God can raise the dead? Yet Paul cannot draw back from writing, 'We also eagerly wait for the Saviour, the Lord Jesus Christ, who will transform our lowly body that it may be conformed to his glorious body, according to the working by which he is able even to subdue all things to himself' (Philippians 3:20-21). Lest we should think that his power to raise the dead is restricted to the bodies of believers, we should recall that he himself said, The hour is coming in which all who are in the graves will hear his voice and come forth—those who have done good, to the resurrection of life, and those who have done evil, to the resurrection of condemnation' (John 5:28-29).

The judge of the world

Following the resurrection, it is Jesus Christ who will judge the world. Solomon wrote, 'God will bring every work into judgement, including every secret thing, whether it is good or whether it is evil' (Ecclesiastes 12:14). But the New Testament insists that 'We must all appear before the judgement seat of Christ' (2 Corinthians 5:10), and that 'He who judges ... is the Lord' (1 Corinthians 4:4). A closer examination of this last verse shows conclusively that 'the Lord' spoken of here is the Lord Jesus Christ. He will come again in glory, and the men and women of all nations will stand before him. As a kingly judge he will separate them one from another, as a shepherd divides his sheep from the goats (Matthew 25:31–46). Nobody will be missing, for we must all appear before him. But in case we should forget who precisely is the Christ before whom we must appear, the apostle puts the same truth elsewhere like this: 'Each of us shall give account of himself to God' (Romans 14:12).

It is true that the one 'ordained by God to be judge of the living and the dead' is a man (Acts 10:42; 17:31). It is true that that man is the Lord Jesus Christ (2 Timothy 4:1). But it is not true that the coming Judge is *only* a man. He is the unique Son of the Father, who has power to save and power to damn (John 5:22,28–29). Even those disobedient to him will call him by his divine title of 'Lord' on that day (Matthew 7:21–23). There will be no veiling of his glory on that fearful occasion (2 Thessalonians 1:7–10). What God alone can do, he will have done. He will have righteously judged the world, and there will not be a being in the whole of his universe who continues to doubt his deity.

After this will come the final dissolution of the universe as we know it, and the renewal of all things. Christ will roll them up like a robe and change them like a garment. But he himself will be unchanged (Hebrews 1:12). Then we will gaze in wonderment at the new heavens and the new earth, and hear his voice from God's throne declaring, 'Behold, I make all things new' (Revelation 21:5).

> He shall reign from pole to pole
> With illimitable sway:
> He shall reign, when, like a scroll,

Yonder heavens have passed away;
Then the end: beneath His rod
Man's last enemy shall fall;
Hallelujah! Christ in God,
God in Christ, is All in all!

James Montgomery, 1771–1854.

Divine worship

If Jesus is God, it cannot be wrong to worship him. The Scriptures teach that not only may worship be given to Christ (as it was, for instance, by Thomas after his resurrection), but that it *should* be given to him.

Such worship is given to him all the time in heaven. Of the Lord Jesus Christ it is commanded: 'Let all the angels of God worship him' (Hebrews 1:6). And they do. Countless myriads surround his throne there, 'saying with a loud voice: "Worthy is the Lamb who was slain to receive power and riches and wisdom, and strength and honour and glory and blessing!"' (Revelation 5:12). These glorious creatures are joined by his people on earth, who exclaim, 'To him who loved us and washed us from our sins in his own blood, and has made us kings and priests to his God and Father, to him be glory and dominion for ever and ever. Amen' (Revelation 1:5–6).

It is because Christians give to Christ their worship that they are known as those who 'call on the name of Jesus Christ' (1 Corinthians 1:2). They do this because God wills that 'all should honour the Son just as they honour the Father'; and they cannot forget that 'He who does not honour the Son does not honour the Father who sent him' (John 5:23), and that 'Whoever denies the Son does not have the Father either; he who acknowledges the Son has the Father also' (1 John 2:23).

This is why Stephen, during his dying moments, offered prayer to the ascended Christ (Acts 7:59–60). This is why the apostle Paul freely prayed to Christ, calling on others to do the same (e.g. Romans 10:12-14; 2 Corinthians 12:8), and held him out as the object of faith (Galatians 2:16; Ephesians 1:15; Philippians 3:8). This is why, as long as the world lasts, converts are to be baptized in the name of the Son, as well as in the name of the Father and of the Holy Spirit (Matthew 28:19). This is why, when the apostle Paul pronounces a benediction on his readers, he invokes the grace of the Lord Jesus Christ, as well as the love of God and the fellowship of the Holy Spirit (2 Corinthians 13:14). The Lord Jesus Christ is God in the same sense as the other two persons.

But at the moment there are many men and women who refuse to worship Christ, as well as an innumerable company of angels—better known as demons—who are in open rebellion against him. Christ has a 'name which is above every name' (Philippians 2:9), but they do not acknowledge it. None the less, the day is coming when all tongues shall acknowledge the supremacy of Christ. This does not mean that all creatures will be saved. Nothing could be further from the truth. Yet, willingly or unwillingly, the whole creation will join together to give homage to Christ and will call him by his divine name. A divine decree makes it certain 'that every tongue [shall] confess that Jesus Christ is Lord, to the glory of God the Father' (Philippians 2:11). All creatures which have ever existed will be agreed on the truth of the deity of Christ.

A common difficulty

Paul's teaching in his Epistle to the Philippians is convincing enough. However, there is another passage by Paul which gives many people a great deal of difficulty. It, too, is a passage about what will transpire at the end of the world. The difficulty arises because the passage, on the face of it, seems to suggest that Christ is inferior to the Father, and somehow less than God. We are, of course, talking about 1 Corinthians 15:22-28, which reads:

> For as in Adam all die, even so in Christ all shall be made alive. But each one in his own order: Christ the first fruits,

afterward those who are Christ's at his coming. Then comes the end, when he delivers the kingdom to God the Father, when he puts an end to all rule and all authority and power. For he must reign till he has put all enemies under his feet. The last enemy that will be destroyed is death. For 'He has put all things under his feet.' But when he says, 'all things are put under him,' it is evident that he who put all things under him is excepted. Now when all things are made subject to him, then the Son himself will also be subject to him who put all things under him, that God may be all in all.

Before we jump to conclusions which are too hasty, we should notice that Paul himself did not consider that his teaching here in any way compromised the deity of Christ. Having given this teaching, he proceeds almost at once to give the divine title of 'Lord' to Christ (v. 31), and then does it four times more before the chapter closes (vv. 47,57,58). In fact he expressly states that the Lord of whom he is writing was not, like Adam, of earthly origin, but is 'the Lord from heaven' (v. 47)—in other words, God become man!

The work of salvation

What then are we to make of the passage we have just quoted? We should call to mind that Paul is showing that the whole work of salvation begins and ends unequivocally with God the Father. Although the Lord Jesus Christ is the Son of God (v. 28), he did not act on his own. God the Father is the Author of salvation, and God the Son is the one by whom it was brought about. To do this he became a man, died, rose and ascended. At his second coming he will put down all enemies that remain in rebellion against God, and then all that he was commissioned to do will have been accomplished. As far as procuring salvation and conquering evil is concerned, there will be nothing further for him to do. At that stage he will, as it were, 'report back' to the Father who sent him. He will hand over to him all his conquests, and it will be seen that God, and not evil, has triumphed. There will be no evil remaining, and nothing anywhere which is not in perfect submission to God. God will be all in all.

But what God did, he did by Christ. Christ did not act for himself, but for the Father who commissioned him. The Son will not give the impression that it was he who triumphed, and that God the Father had nothing to do with it. So when Christ has brought everything else to submit to God, he will submit himself to him, and do him homage. It will be clear that Christ's work was not done in isolation. He did not do it without reference to the Father. All that has been accomplished has been done by means of an unbroken harmony between the three persons of the Trinity.

Order but not ranks

We are making a grave mistake if we conclude from all this that God the Son is somehow less than God the Father. We have already seen in this book that the eternal generation of the Son in no way implies inferiority. The fact that there is an order in the Godhead does not mean that there are any ranks. Priority does not imply superiority. I have pursued this point more fully in *The Three Are One* and, as this particular book is not about the whole doctrine of the Trinity, need only to mention it here. But it needs to be stressed that the eternal relationship between the Father and the Son in no way suggests that one is senior and the other junior. Certainly the order that exists within the Godhead is reflected outwardly in the way that God acts. What the Father does, he always does by Christ. As Mediator, Christ does not act in his own right, although he is God in his own right. Mortal minds can never grasp all this, but it remains, none the less, what the Bible teaches.

However, we must never forget that what Christ did, he did as a man. He became a man in Mary's womb, and remains a man today and for ever. We shall pursue this theme in the second section of this book, but it is important to recall these facts when considering the passage that we have in mind. The Mediator who 'reports back' to the Father is a man, albeit he is as much God as the Father. Can a man be in the presence of God and be unsubmissive to him, even though that man is the God-Man? If we think this through, the passage will now present us with few remaining difficulties. We will certainly no longer consider that it militates against our believing in the deity of our Saviour. How could Paul assert *with certainty* that all enemies will at last be under Christ's feet, if Christ was in any way less than God himself?

The necessity of his Godhead

As we close this first section of this book, it is clear to us that the Bible certainly teaches the deity of Christ. We gladly repeat the truth: he is God eternally; he was God while among us; and he is God now and always. How grateful we should be that this truth is so clearly taught in God's Word! Our whole salvation depends on it.

If Jesus had been less than God, he would still be dead in his tomb. No mere man, however perfect, and however wonderfully endued with the Holy Spirit, could have successfully made the claim of John 10:17: 'Therefore my Father loves me, because I lay down my life that I may take it again.' A mere man may, in a sense, be said to lay down his life, but he must be more than a mere man to take it up again. To be subject to death and yet sovereign over it, the man who dies must also be God. If our Lord Jesus Christ had not been God, we would have no living Saviour today. We would have nowhere to turn. We would still be in our sins and rushing guiltily to eternal damnation.

But let us think of his life and death which preceded his resurrection. Who but God himself could have rendered perfect obedience to the law of God, and then have died as a sacrifice of infinite value on behalf of countless others? Because he was God he was able to offer that which is greater in value than is required by the sins of the whole world. If he had not been God, and thus infinite in capacity for suffering, how could he have suffered the limitless wrath of God in but a few hours at Golgotha? Who but the infinite God himself could have paid the penalty which the infinite God demanded?

God himself came to redeem us. What love! But he came as a man, and the humanity of the Saviour is as essential to our salvation as his deity. It is to this truth that we now turn.

> Jesus, we ne'er can pay
> The debt we owe Thy love;
> Yet tell us how we may
> Our gratitude approve:
> Our hearts, our all, to Thee we give,
> The gift, though small, do Thou receive.
>
> Samuel Stennett, 1727–1795.

Jesus—his humanity

4

The promise of a man

We have seen that our Lord Jesus Christ was God from eternity, that he continued to be God throughout the period of his incarnation, and that he is God now and for ever. In the second section of this book we come to reflect on the fact that the eternal Son of God became man. He continues to be a man to this day, and will always be one. He is both God and man, in two distinct natures.

Our Lord did not become a man until he was conceived by the power of the Holy Spirit in the womb of the virgin Mary. But even before that time it was plain that the Son of God would one day take to himself a human nature. Indeed, several times before his incarnation, and as a pledge of it, he actually *appeared* as a man!

The Angel of the Lord

This last statement cannot be supported by simply quoting an Old Testament passage or two. To demonstrate it, it is necessary to engage in a careful comparison of quite a large number of Scripture passages.

We should begin by looking at those Old Testament passages which refer to 'the Angel of the Lord'. It is quite plain that this person is God himself. It is equally plain that he is to be distinguished from God. The word 'angel' means 'messenger' or 'one sent', and the phrase 'the Angel of the Lord' therefore means 'the One sent by Jehovah'.

Genesis 16:7–13 records how Hagar, who had run away from Abram and Sarai, was commanded by 'the Angel of the Lord' to return. It is then made clear that it was the Lord himself who was speaking to her, and she responded by calling him 'You-are-the-God-who-sees'. The one who was sent by God, and who took a visible form before her, was none other than God himself!

Abraham

Abraham himself had a visit from the Angel of the Lord some time later, in the plains of Mamre (Genesis 18). The visitor is specifically said to have appeared as a man (v. 2), but it is also clearly stated that it was the Lord himself (vv. 1,13–14). Abraham recognized this and offered prayer to him (vv. 23–33). He stood before a man, and addressed him as God!

This was not the last time that Abraham was to meet the Angel of the Lord. It was none other than the Angel who stopped him from slaying his son Isaac (Genesis 22:11–15). Abraham called the name of the place 'The-Lord-will-provide' (v. 14), for once more he clearly recognized the identity of the heavenly visitor. The Angel gave him a promise, which began, 'By myself I have sworn, says the Lord …' (v. 16). The one whom the Lord sent *was* the Lord!

Moses

There are many other references to the Angel in the Old Testament, and on each occasion it is plain that God's messenger, who is so often specifically said to be in human form, is God. It is 'the Angel of the Lord' who speaks to Moses from the burning bush and says, 'I am the God of your father …' (Exodus 3:6), and goes on to reveal his names as 'I am who I am' (v. 14). The voice of the Angel was 'the voice of the Lord' (Acts 7:31). That Angel is the God who led Jacob and redeemed him (Genesis 48:15–16), and is the Lord himself who went before the Israelites as they fled from Egypt (Exodus 13:21; 14:19). It is the Angel of the Lord who appears twice in the book of Judges, and on each occasion reveals that he is God himself (Judges 6:11,12,14,16; 13:3,9,22). But his visible form was evidently that of a man, because we read that he 'sat' (6:11), 'looked' (6:14, AV) and had a 'countenance' (13:6). On both occasions he looked so obviously like a man that those who met him brought him meals (6:19–22; 13:15–23). The one they spoke of as 'a Man of God' and 'the Man' (13:6,10) was God, *sent* by God! Who else could this have been but the pre-incarnate and eternal Son of God?

Jacob

The Old Testament takes pains to underline that this person who appeared as a man was not God in any secondary sense. It does this in a variety of ways. For instance, in Jacob's famous dream of a ladder reaching to heaven, it states: 'Behold, the LORD stood above it and said: "I am the LORD God of Abraham your father and the God of Isaac …"' (Genesis 28:13). The point is made. Jacob saw God. The statement is made without qualification. It is only much later in the narrative, when Jacob is giving his account of another dream, that the identity of God as the Angel of God is made: 'Then the Angel of God spoke to me in a dream, saying … "I am the God of Bethel …"' (Genesis 31:11,13). In this way the idea that the angel he saw was in any way less than God is totally destroyed.

On another occasion 'Jacob was left alone; and a Man wrestled with him until the breaking of day' (Genesis 32:24). The identity of this man is not revealed to us straight away, until Jacob's own testimony drives it into our minds with considerable force: 'And Jacob called the name of the place Peniel [i.e. The face of God]: "For I have seen God face to face, and my life is preserved"' (Genesis 32:30). Long before Christ's incarnation Jacob wrestled with a man who turned out to be God! 'Yes, he struggled with the Angel and prevailed; he wept, and sought favour from him. He found him in Bethel, and there he spoke to us—that is, the LORD God of hosts. The LORD is his memorial' (Hosea 12:4-5).

Similarly, when the law of God was given to the Israelite nation on Mount Sinai, God himself spoke there in an audible voice, in human language (Deuteronomy 4:33,36,39). 'You came down also on Mount Sinai, and spoke with them from heaven, and gave them just ordinances and true laws, good statutes and commandments' (Nehemiah 9:13). The Old Testament baldly states that the voice which spoke was the voice of God. It is not until Stephen's great speech of defence in the New Testament that we are specifically told that the voice which gave the law was that of 'the Angel' (Acts 7:38). We need never doubt that the Angel of the LORD is Jehovah himself. The Angel of his presence' is none other than the LORD (Isaiah 63:7–9).

The Angel identified

What shall we make of all this? In the references we have cited, God was certainly seen in a visible and human form. How does this tie up with the New Testament's assertion that 'No one has seen God at any time'? (John 1:18).

The answer is clear when we read the whole of that verse. It reads, 'No one has seen God at any time. The only begotten Son, who is in the bosom of the Father, he has declared him.' When John says that nobody has seen God, he means that nobody has seen God the Father. This is confirmed by John 6:46: 'Not that anyone has seen the Father.' No one has seen God the Father. None the less, human eyes have seen *God*! The God they have seen is God the Son. He is the one who said, 'The Father has sent me' (John 5:36). There is one who is God, who has been *sent* by God. That is who 'the Angel of the LORD' was. The eternal Son of God appeared many times in human form long before he took to himself a real human nature.

Every visible appearance of God has been an appearance of the Lord Jesus Christ. The glory of God is seen nowhere else but in his face (2 Corinthians 4:6). But no one must think that he has missed out in some way, because he has not seen God the Father.

Jesus stands before the world and announces, 'I and my Father are one' (John 10:30); 'He who sees me sees him who sent me' (John 12:45); 'He who has seen me has seen the Father; so how can you say, "Show us the Father"?' (John 14:9).

We remind ourselves again that when Isaiah saw Jehovah in all his glory and prostrated himself in the presence of his overbearing holiness, it was the Lord Jesus Christ that he saw (compare Isaiah 6:1-12 with John 12:39-41). The God that he saw in that majestic vision was in the form of a man! He was sitting on a lofty throne, and the train of his robe filled the temple. We may assume that this experience was not much different from that of Moses and Aaron and the elders of Israel, when they 'saw the God of Israel' and ate and drank in his presence (Exodus 24:9-10). But why should God, whose essence is invisible, manifest himself through his Son in human form, even in Old Testament times?

To come as a man

The answer is that we may regard Christ's pre-incarnate appearances in human form as pledges of his eventual coming among men in human nature.

Zechariah

This is confirmed by examining a number of other Old Testament verses. For instance, in Zechariah 2:10-11 we meet the same concept of Jehovah sending someone who is himself Jehovah. In the light of what we now know about 'the Angel of the Lord', we no longer find such language extraordinary. But this time there is an additional factor. On this occasion the Lord who is sent promises to 'dwell' among his people. Seeing that when he appeared to his people he *appeared* as a man, is it not a logical transition of thought to expect that when he comes to dwell among them he will come to *dwell* as a man? When Zechariah wrote, no incarnation had yet taken place. But the expectancy of it was excited by his writing. He prepared the way, and never more powerfully than when he wrote so boldly of Jehovah's Shepherd, described by the Lord of hosts as 'the *man* who is my companion' (Zechariah 13:7, emphasis mine). Did Peter have this verse in mind when he explained that the Old Testament prophets did not fully understand what was revealed to them about the coming Christ? (1 Peter 1:10-11). Whether Zechariah himself understood his prophecy or not, it is clear enough to those of us who look back on it. The first step, that of the Son of God *appearing* as a man, would be followed by a second. He would *become* man.

In declaring this truth, Zechariah was not a lonely voice. Before his day Micah had already written that he 'whose goings forth have been from of old, from everlasting' would come from Bethlehem, as Israel's ruler (Micah 5:2). The Jews rightly understood this as a prediction that the one spoken of would be *born* there (Matthew 2:1-8; John 7:42). What they completely failed to realize was that the person who would thus enter the human race would be none less than *the everlasting God!* Had they understood this, they would not have persecuted and crucified the Lord of glory. As it was, the truth was hidden from them. The Scriptures testified of Christ (John 5:39-40), but the Jews neither understood them, nor God's power. They therefore inevitably remained in their errors and would not come to him (Matthew 22:29).

Micah

Micah's ministry took place at the same time as that of Isaiah. He too wrote of the coming Messiah, and in fact wrote more about him than any other Old Testament writer. We have already studied what he wrote concerning the Son to be born of a virgin (Isaiah 7:14). We stressed how that prediction revealed the *deity* of the coming Messiah. But we should now take time to notice that it was equally a prediction that God would be *born*. It was followed by a further prediction, revealing that the coming Messiah would grace Galilee, and that he would flood it with spiritual light. He would be the mighty God, who would occupy David's throne. Yet he would come as a child born, and as a son (Isaiah 9:1–7; Matthew 4:14–16). This was the astonishing work which God's power was about to perform. God was going to visit the human race *as one of that race*!

All this teaching is so clear that we can only explain the Jews' failure to see it on the grounds that they were spiritually blind. The passages of Scripture to which we have referred were not obscure. The Jews knew all of them well. But they simply did not see what these passages were saying. They expected a Messiah, but not one who would be God. They never grasped the stupendous assertions of Scripture that God would be *born*: that God would come among men as a man.

Did the question put by our Lord in Matthew 22:43–44 never cross their minds until it was raised by him? All Jews knew that the coming Messiah would be David's 'son' or descendant. All of them took Psalm 110 to be about that Messiah. If there had not been universal agreement on this point, the apostle's arguments based on this passage, found in Hebrews 5:6 and 7:17, would have had no force whatever. But Psalm 110 was by David. If the Messiah was to be David's descendant, how could David refer to him as 'Lord'? The answer is, of course, that the human descendant would be divine. God was going to come into the world as the human descendant of David. Here was as clear an indication of the coming incarnation of the Son of God as anyone could have hoped to have found. But the Jews just did not see it.

If they could not see the truth enshrined in Psalm 110, could they not see it in Psalm 2, which they sang so often? Did it not tell them that he who is in heaven has set on earth his appointed king (human) who is his Son (divine)? (Psalm 2:6,7,10–12). Did not that psalm tell them that to serve God's Son was to serve the Lord? Could they not have discerned from the psalm sufficient spiritual truth to lead them to expect a divine Messiah who would be truly a man?

Malachi

Added to these voices was that of Malachi. It was his voice, as we have seen, which closed the Old Testament canon, and echoed across the four-century gap between the Testaments, until its theme was taken up by John the Baptist.

Malachi faithfully recorded God's words: '"Behold, I send my messenger, and he will prepare the way before me. And the Lord, whom you seek, will suddenly come to his temple, even the messenger of the covenant, in whom you delight. Behold, he is coming," says the LORD of hosts' (Malachi 3:1). Confronted by John's claim to be the fulfilment of the first part of this verse, the whole of Israel should have been filled with expectancy. Happily, a lot of people were (Mark 1:1–9). For the next event was to be the actual *coming* of the 'Angel' or 'Messenger' of the covenant. He who had so often *appeared* as a man, was actually to *visit* the nation, and to come to his temple. The fact of his coming is stated twice. What else could Malachi have meant other than that 'the Angel' should physically come to his temple as a man? The first messenger of the verse was obviously a man. How could it be argued that the second was going to be anything different?

Really a man

These verses, which stress that the coming God will be a man and that the coming man will be God, are not the only verses in the Old Testament about the coming Messiah. Looking back, we see clearly that all the ancient prophets were 'searching what, or what manner of time, the Spirit of Christ who was in them was indicating when he testified beforehand the sufferings of Christ and the glories that would follow' (1 Peter 1:11). They gave detail after detail about the coming Christ. Several of these, as we have seen, revealed that the coming one was God. All of them underlined that he would really be a *man*. None of the following predictions would have made any sense if this were not so.

As to the time of his coming, it was predicted that it would be before the sceptre departed from Judah (Genesis 49:10), at the end of four hundred and ninety years after the going forth of the command to rebuild Jerusalem (Daniel 9:24-27) and while the second temple was still standing (Haggai 2:9; Malachi 3:1).

He was to experience human birth (Isaiah 7:14; 9:6; Genesis 3:15; 17:7), and to be born in a low condition (Psalm 22:6,9-12; Micah 5:2), and would be of the tribe of Judah and of the family of David (Jeremiah 23:5-6). We have already seen that he was to be born of a virgin (Isaiah 7:14) and preceded by a forerunner (Malachi 3:1). He would be subject to God's law and would render perfect obedience to it (Psalm 40:6-10). At last he would die, would be buried and would continue under the power of death for a time (Isaiah 53; Psalm 16:9-11; 118:17-23; 22).

Many of the details of his death, and the events leading up to it, are predicted in finer detail. He would enter the city riding upon an ass (Zechariah 9:9). He was to be sold for thirty pieces of silver and the price was to be used to purchase a potter's field (Zechariah 11:12-13). He was to be whipped, tortured, spat upon and humiliated (Isaiah 50:6). His garments were to be parted by lot (Psalm 22:18). He was to be given vinegar to drink (Psalm 69:21). The very words he was to utter from the cross were predicted (Psalm 22:1), as was the fact that his bones would be dislocated there (as happened in all crucifixions) (Psalm 22:14). He would be pierced (Psalm 22:16; Zechariah 12:10), scoffed at (Psalm 22:7-8), stared at (Psalm 22:17), and associated with both the wicked and the rich in his death (Isaiah 53:9).

We say it again, 1 Peter 1:10-11 leads us to believe that the prophets did not themselves understand everything that they wrote about the coming Messiah. But the predictions were made, none the less. And if all the details could not be discerned before the time, at least those who had eyes to see were not in doubt about one great fact. When he came, he would be no phantom. He really would be a *man*.

To the name of our salvation,
Laud and honour let us pay,
Which for many a generation
Hid in God's foreknowledge lay,
But with holy exultation
We may sing aloud today.

Jesus is the name we treasure,
Name beyond what words can tell;
Name of gladness, name of pleasure,
Ear and heart delighting well;
Name of sweetness passing measure,
Saving us from sin and hell.

'Tis the name that whoso preacheth
Speaks like music to the ear;
Who in prayer this name beseecheth
Sweetest comfort findeth near;
Who its perfect wisdom reacheth,
Heavenly joy possesseth here.

Jesus is the name exalted
Over every other name;
In this name, whene'er assaulted,
We can put our foes to shame:
Strength to them who else had halted,
Eyes to blind, and feet to lame.

Therefore we in love adoring
This most blessed name revere,
Holy Jesu, Thee imploring
So to write it in us here
That, hereafter heavenward soaring,
We may sing with angels there.

Anonymous, 15th century.
Translated by John Mason Neale, 1818–1866.

5

Behold the man!

The Lord Jesus Christ, without ceasing to be God, became man. What was foreshadowed and pledged in the Old Testament became a historical fact. He assumed human nature, bore the human likeness and was revealed in human form. He carried a human name—Jesus of Nazareth.

'Men have sometimes forgotten the human Christ in their reverence for the divine. It is very important to maintain the reality and integrity of the humanity of Jesus by admitting his human development and human limitations. The splendour of His deity should not be stressed to the extent of obscuring His real humanity.' Thus wrote Louis Berkhof. It is to this question of the reality and integrity of the humanity of Jesus that we now give our attention.

Virgin birth

The eternal Son of God entered the human race by the womb of the virgin Mary. 'When the fulness of the time had come, God sent forth his Son, born of a woman' (Galatians 4:4).

Jesus had no human father. He was conceived by the power of the Holy Spirit in Mary's womb (Matthew 1:20). The Holy Spirit came upon her and the power of the Highest overshadowed her. Her baby was a holy child who was none other than the Son of

God (Luke 1:35). The virgin conception, predicted long before by Isaiah, had at last come to pass! (Isaiah 7:14; Matthew 1:23). Here was the fulfilment of the oft-repeated promises that God himself would one day visit and redeem his people.

The supernatural operation of the Holy Spirit in Mary's womb, excluding the necessity for the activity of a man, was entirely in harmony with the fact that the person who was born was the eternal Son of God. The Spirit's activity sanctified the human nature of Christ from its very inception, and thus kept it free from the pollution of sin which plagues every other member of the human race. We cannot say exactly how the Holy Spirit did this. Nobody knows precisely how the pollution of sin is passed from parent to child. But we should take note that the sanctifying influence of the Holy Spirit did not operate only at his conception. It continued throughout his life (John 3:34; Hebrews 9:14).

Christ's being born of a woman was a wonderful fulfilment of the first promise of a Messiah in Genesis, and gave him a true human nature. His being born of God displayed and underlined that his was a divine nature, and that his birth was not the beginning of his existence. His birth did not contain any element of subtraction. We saw in chapter 2 that he was as much the Son of God, co-equal with the Father, after his incarnation as before. But it did contain the element of *addition*. He became what he previously was not. He took to himself a human nature and entered the human race, without sharing in its awful guilt and corruption.

Truly a man

We must never be tempted to think that because Christ's conception was supernatural, his human nature was therefore less than real. Sin apart, he became one of us. 'Inasmuch then as the children have partaken of flesh and blood, he himself likewise shared in the same … For indeed he does not give aid to angels, but he does give aid to the seed of Abraham. Therefore, in all things he had to be made like his brethren' (Hebrews 2:14–17).

The Gospel records lean over backwards, as it were, to make us understand that our Lord Jesus Christ, although fully God, as we have seen, had a true human nature. He was *more* than a man, it is true. But his humanity was real. It was the same as ours. There was nothing unreal, imaginary or merely apparent about it. We say it again, he became one of *us*.

A baby was born to a Galilean girl—a baby of whom the evangelists have carefully recorded the ancestry (Matthew 1:1–17; Luke 3:23–38; Acts 13:23; see John 7:27). He was wrapped in swaddling clothes and laid in a manger (Luke 2:7). This is all that the visiting shepherds saw, although an angelic announcement had assured them that the baby was 'a Saviour, who is Christ the Lord' (Luke 2:8–20).

There was nothing unreal about the small boy's circumcision, which took place on the eighth day of his life; nor about his presentation in the temple, where old Simeon lifted him in his arms (Luke 2:21–35). There was nothing unreal about the toddler visited by wise men from the East, who had to be taken into Egypt to escape from the malice of Herod the Great (Matthew 2:1–23). There was nothing unreal about the boy who later grew up in the carpenter's house in Nazareth. He grew and developed like the other boys in the village—but there was something noticeably different about him: 'The child grew and became strong in spirit, filled with wisdom; and the grace of God was upon him' (Luke 2:40).

It was a real boy who travelled up to Jerusalem when he was twelve years old, who worried Joseph and Mary by his disappearance and who, three days later, was found in the temple listening to the theological teachers and asking them questions. It is true that he was conscious that his only Father was God, but this in no way lessened the reality of his return to his home in Nazareth, his submission to parental authority there, and the fact that he 'increased in wisdom and stature, and in favour with God and men' (Luke 2:41–52). It is only because he was as human as the other members of his family that the incredulous inhabitants of Nazareth were later able to ask of the miracle-working Teacher, 'Is this not the carpenter, the son of Mary, and brother of James, Joses, Judas, and Simon? And are not his sisters here with us?' (Mark 6:3).

It was a man that John the Baptist baptized in the Jordan, although many aspects of the event testified that Christ was the eternal Son of God (John 1:30; Matthew 3:13–17). Christ's baptism marked the beginning of his public ministry. This had a mixed reception, but met with outright hostility from those who knew him best. When they discovered that he had actually gathered a band of disciples around him, their reaction was to try and restrain him from embarking on a career as a travelling teacher. To them the project was foolhardy, and they insisted that he was mad (Mark 3:21). Could they have done and said this if they had not been perfectly convinced that Jesus of Nazareth was as much a man as themselves? Could his enemies have maliciously called him 'a gluttonous man and a winebibber' if they had not been entirely certain of his humanity? (Matthew 11:19).

The self-consciousness of Jesus

But it was not just others who were conscious of Jesus' humanity. He was conscious of it himself. In chapter 2 we pointed out that he was aware of his divine identity. We have just seen again that even as a boy he knew that God was his only Father. He carried a similar consciousness as far as his humanity was concerned. He went through life with the human awareness that he who was uniquely his Father was greater than he was (John 14:28).

Jesus often referred to himself as a man. Far from raising any objection to the idea, he was conscious of it all the time. To the Jews who viciously opposed him, he said, 'If you were Abraham's children, you would do the works of Abraham. But now you seek to kill me, a *man* who has told you the truth which I heard from God. Abraham did not do this' (John 8:39–40, emphasis mine). It was also referring to his opponents that he said, 'If I had not done among them the works which none other *man* did, they had not had sin: but now have they both seen and hated both me and my Father' (John 15:24, AV, emphasis mine).

There was no tension in the mind of Jesus between being conscious of his heavenly origin and being conscious of his manhood. Once we realize this, we can begin to understand how he could make the following statements: 'No one has ascended to heaven but he who came down from heaven, that is, the Son of Man who is in heaven' (John 3:13). 'What then if you should see the Son of Man ascend where he was before?' (John 6:62).

The Son of Man

Jesus' use of the title 'Son of Man' in these verses, and in eighty other places in the Gospels, is particularly interesting. It was his favourite way of referring to himself, but was a designation hardly ever used of him by others. Whenever he thought of himself, he thought of 'the Son of Man'. 'The Son of Man is Lord even of the sabbath' he said of himself (Matthew 12:8). 'The Son of Man has come to seek and to save that which was lost' (Luke 19:10). His use of this title gives us a unique insight into the self-consciousness of Jesus. It shows us what was in his mind when he was the object of his own thoughts.

There has been considerable discussion as to why Jesus described himself in this way. The title was obviously very full of meaning for him. Some think that he chose this title from the book of Daniel in the Old Testament, where God's kingdom is pictorially represented by one like 'the Son of Man' (Daniel 7:13). If this is so, Jesus was probably using the title to show that he was the Messiah whom the Old Testament predicted, but not the Messiah which popular Jewish opinion had come to expect. To have used the word 'Messiah' of himself would have excited their hopes in the wrong direction, because they had already loaded the word with their own interpretation. By using the unusual title 'Son of Man' he avoided this danger completely, and they had to listen more carefully to his own definition of his rôle.

But Daniel was not the only person in the Old Testament to use this expression. It is found in Psalm 8:4 and Psalm 146:3, but also very frequently in the prophecy of Ezekiel. Again and again God calls the prophet 'son of man'. The purpose seems to be that of putting Ezekiel in his rightful place before the majesty of God. Compared with God's glory, Ezekiel's position is one of insignificance. Confronted with unveiled Deity, he must understand his feebleness and mere humanity. If Jesus used this expression of himself in this sense, it must be because he spent his days among us aware of the glory from which he had come, and equally aware of the lowliness and humiliation of the state which he had come to occupy.

It is possible that Jesus had both senses of his title in his mind. He was aware that he was the King of God's kingdom, and that that kingdom would be established by his humiliation. Whatever may be the exact balance of truth in this matter, there is no doubt that the title 'Son of Man' perfectly sets forth the fact that Jesus was a true man. Whatever else he may have intended by his use of the title, he was aware of *that*.

Obviously a man

The self-consciousness of Jesus regarding his humanity was fully borne out by what others saw of him during his public ministry. He was *obviously* a man.

For a start, he looked like a man. What else would we expect of him who was 'the son of David' and the fruit of his loins? He came 'in the likeness of sinful flesh' (Romans 8:3). The woman of Samaria noticed nothing unusual about his appearance. As far as she was concerned, she had been engaged in conversation by just one more hated Jew (John 4:9). His physical appearance was so unstriking, so like that of other men, that he could walk the streets of Jerusalem quite unrecognized until he attracted attention by going to the temple to preach publicly (John 7:10–14). So indistinguishable was he from others that it was necessary for his betrayer actually to kiss him to make sure that those who had come to arrest him did not lay hands on the wrong person (Matthew 26:47–50). Even after his resurrection two disciples walking to Emmaus took him to be simply a fellow-citizen who was not quite up-to-date with the news (Luke 24:18–19). Mary thought that he was the gardener who looked after the area surrounding her Lord's tomb (John 20:15). Those who had known him for years did not see any significant difference between him and any other Galilean man who might have been standing by the lakeside (John 21:4–5). We must abandon all ideas that Jesus' face shone, or that he was surrounded by a halo. Even after his resurrection there was nothing unnatural or less than human about the physical appearance of Jesus of Nazareth.

Common experiences

But we stress that Christ's humanity was not just a matter of appearance. The Gospels bring out in detail that the common experiences of other men and women were his too. Like every other person, he hungered (Matthew 4:2; Mark 11:12; Matthew 21:18). But God does not hunger (Psalm 50:12). He was thirsty (John 4:7; 19:28, the second of these references being a fulfilment of Psalm 69:21). He knew what it was to be tired (John 4:6), although God is never weary (Isaiah 40:28). He fell asleep (Matthew 8:24). But God never slumbers nor sleeps (Psalm 121:4). At these points he did what every man and woman does, but what God never does. He obviously had a nature *additional* to the divine nature which we have seen he possessed. That other nature was a human one.

On occasions the disciples heard Christ speak of his body (e.g. Luke 7:44–46). He spoke beforehand of its burial (Mark 14:8; Matthew 26:12). It was on that body that John leaned during the last supper (John 13:23), where Jesus spoke of it again (Matthew 26:26). There was nothing unreal about the human nature of the Lord with whom they reclined at table that night. They had seen him eating and drinking on other occasions (Matthew 9:10–13;

11:19), and they spent that sad evening watching him doing it again, as he used the bread and wine as symbols of what was about to happen to him.

Suffering

Within hours they were watching him suffer. He had suffered throughout his life, but this was the climax. He had known what it was to experience the repeated assaults of Satan, the hatred and unbelief of his own people and the persecution of his enemies. But now his sufferings knew their deepest severity. It was no phantom who was 'in agony', whose 'sweat became like great drops of blood falling down to the ground' (Luke 22:44). It was no phantom who was made 'perfect through sufferings' and who 'learned obedience by the things which he suffered' (Hebrews 2:10; 5:8). It was no phantom who 'suffered for us in the flesh' and was 'put to death in the flesh' (1 Peter 4:1; 3:18). His human body was real. No wonder Pilate paraded him before the waiting crowd and cried, 'Behold the man!' (John 19:5).

And so at last Jesus Christ died—although God cannot die. He bowed his head and released his spirit (John 19:30). He was obedient to death, even the death of the cross (Philippians 2:8). Shortly afterwards the soldiers, to be entirely certain that he was dead, pierced his side with a spear. John himself witnessed the pouring out of blood and water from the wound, which followed (John 19:32–35). A little later his limp corpse was taken by Nicodemus and Joseph of Arimathaea, and wound in linen clothes impregnated with preserving aromatics and spices (John 19:38–42). It was then laid in Joseph's rock-hewn tomb, where it remained until the glorious Sunday morning of his resurrection.

The disciples were in despair. The Lord Jesus Christ was so obviously a man that, when he died, they grieved that he was no longer with them. When the body was known to be missing from the grave, Mary's heart broke because 'They have taken away my Lord, and I do not know where they have laid him' (John 20:13). To her, the body was *him*! She and all his other disciples would have laughed to scorn the suggestion that his body was somehow less real than other people's, or was a mere appearance without any real substance. Jesus was fully a man, and they knew it. When his body was no longer alive, they thought that they had lost him. When his body was gone, their grief could not be contained. All that they had ever known him to be was in that body.

How overjoyed they were when the resurrection restored their Lord to them! His physical appearance was as human as before. They heard him speak of himself as 'flesh and bones' (Luke 24:39). They clung to him (John 20:17), handled him (Luke 24:39), examined his wounds (Luke 24:39; John 20:27), watched him cook (John 21:9–14) and saw him eat (Luke 24:42). He had conquered death. But he who had conquered death was still obviously *a* man!

Not just a body

Our Lord's having a true human body was a fundamental part of God's plan (Hebrews 10:5). But having a body is only part of what it means to be truly human. There is an invisible side to human nature as well. Did the eternal Son of God merely animate the molecular structure of a human frame, or was he a true man, body and soul? Was his humanity merely partial? Or was it total?

The Bible's answer is clear. Our Lord did not just have a human body. He had a complete human nature. In addition to his physical body there was an invisible side to his human make-up. He had a soul. He had a human spirit.

The final proof of this was his death. Death was for him what it is for every man. It was the separation of body and spirit. He released his spirit into his Father's care, and immediately his human body hung dead upon the cross (Luke 23:46). The event demonstrated conclusively that his humanity was composed of the two constituent elements which make real humanity.

A human soul

But we do not have to wait to read of his death to realize that our Lord had a human soul. On several occasions he spoke of his soul, and in particular of the distress which his human spirit was experiencing—especially when he contemplated his cross and considered the tragedy of his certain betrayal. There are indications in those references that our Lord craved human sympathy, and it would be hard to find a more decisive proof of the existence of a truly human spirit than that (John 12:27; 13:21; Matthew 26:38; Mark 14:34; Luke 22:44; see also John 15:14–15).

As a consequence of having a human spirit, our Lord had a human will. How else could he have prayed, 'O my Father, if it is possible, let this cup pass from me; nevertheless, not as I will, but as you will'? (Matthew 26:39). His human will was not at variance with the divine will at any point. But it was a separate will for all that, as the verse above so decisively reveals.

Increase in wisdom and stature

That our Lord's humanity was not limited to a mere physical resemblance is a fact made clear almost from the beginning of the Gospel narratives. As the young boy grew in Nazareth, Luke also records that he 'became strong in spirit, filled with wisdom' (Luke 2:40). On the brink of adolescence he 'increased in wisdom and stature' (Luke 2:52). Side by side with his physical development ran his development as a person. He acquired his knowledge through the ordinary channels open to the other boys of his day. He listened to Joseph and Mary, and to his teachers, and studied and reflected. At the same time the inner qualities of his character became more and more apparent. Particularly striking was his startling wisdom, which became greater every day. Although he was the omniscient God, our human Lord was subject to human limitations, and went through the normal processes of human development. He was seen to make progress. The mystery of this truth is unfathomable, but the fact is none the less recorded. The process never ceased during his lifetime, and even in full maturity there were certain things of which he, as a man, was ignorant (Mark 13:32). Each experience of life advanced him further in the way of obedience (Hebrews 5:8) and more fully equipped him to be the captain of our salvation (Hebrews 2:10). None of this could be true if he had not been a true man. None of this could be true if he had not had a human soul and spirit.

Emotional life

Further evidence of our Lord's soul is seen in the fact that he had a human emotional life. He knew what it was to be glad, and 'rejoiced in the Spirit' as he reflected that God reveals himself to those whom the world despises (Luke 10:21). He knew what it was to shed tears. With an aching human spirit he wept outside Lazarus' tomb (John 11:33–36). 'Vehement cries and tears' were part of his human experience, and not least when he considered the certain and horrific massacre of the impenitent inhabitants of Jerusalem (Hebrews 5:7; Luke 19:41–44).

On occasions our Lord was 'moved with compassion' (Matthew 9:36) and his human soul revealed itself in pity and sympathy. On other occasions he was grieved and angry (Mark 3:5; 10:14). He knew what it was to have a special affection for some people (Mark 10:21), and nowhere was this more evident than in the fact that he took particular pleasure in being in one little home in Bethany (John 11:5). Most human of all, he knew what it was to be tempted (Matthew 4:1–11). The last Adam was not exempt from what the first Adam experienced. The great difference was that he did not yield to temptation (Hebrews 4:15). We ought to notice that if our Lord had not had a true human spirit, it would have been impossible for him to have been tempted. God cannot be tempted (James 1:13). A human body merely taken over by the Godhead could not have had this experience. It was only because our Lord was a man body and soul that the devil could approach him in this way.

Prayer

And how was the human spirit of our Lord sustained during these times of temptation and during the other great crises of his life? The New Testament narratives emphasize that his whole ministry as a man could not have taken place if it had not been for the supporting power of the Holy Spirit (see Luke 10:21; Hebrews 9:14). This support for his spiritual life became his by prayer and communion with his Father. He needed to pray, just as we need to pray (Mark 1:35), and he set aside special times to do so when particular guidance was needed (e.g. Luke 5:16; 6:12; 9:18,28). Would Jesus have needed to pray if he had not had a fully human spirit and soul like ours? Indeed, if he had been simply a human frame devoid of human spirit, and merely 'inhabited' by Deity, would he even have been capable of prayer? Is not prayer communion between a human spirit and God, who is a Spirit? If there was no spirit in Christ which was separate from the divine Spirit, prayer would have been impossible for him.

The Apostles' affirmation

Our Lord, then, was a man through and through. No wonder that the New Testament writers have no embarrassment in calling him such. Far from shying away from the idea, or diverting attention from it, they proclaim it over and over again.

At Pentecost Peter speaks of Christ as 'a man attested by God' (Acts 2:22). Paul, at Antioch, announces to the Jews 'that through this man is preached to you the forgiveness of sins' (Acts 13:38). To the scoffing intellectuals of Athens he gives the assurance that God 'has appointed a day on which he will judge the world in righteousness by the man whom he has ordained' (Acts 17:31). To the believers at Corinth he gives the teaching that 'By man came ... the resurrection of the dead' (1 Corinthians 15:21), while elsewhere Jesus is referred to simply as 'this man' (Hebrews 8:3, AV; 10:10–12). The real humanity of the Lord Jesus Christ was part and parcel of the gospel message proclaimed by the apostles.

In the light of what we have learned we must understand the references to Christ coming in 'the flesh' not simply as statements that he had a human body, but that he took to himself a true human nature, in its completeness. This is the ultimate mystery of the incarnation. 'The Word became flesh' (John 1:14); 'God was manifested in the flesh' (1 Timothy 3:16); 'Jesus Christ has come in the flesh' (1 John 4:2); 'Inasmuch then as the children have partaken of flesh and blood, he himself likewise shared in the same' (Hebrews 2:14).

Any denial of this truth is heresy. This is because if the Son of God did not take to himself a true human nature, there is no salvation for us, and we have no gospel to preach. We shall come back to this point. But it needs to be stated now. Those who deny the true humanity of the Lord Jesus Christ are as much the enemies of his gospel as those who deny his deity. This is a point which the New Testament is at pains to underline (see 1 John 2:22–25; 4:1–6; 5:5–12; 2 John 7,9–11). 'Every spirit that does not confess that Jesus Christ has come in the flesh is not of God. And this is the spirit of the antichrist, which you have heard was coming, and is now already in the world' (1 John 4:3).

A sinless man

In saying that Jesus had a complete human nature, we must never let our minds slip into the error of thinking that he had a sinful nature. It is true that he came 'in the likeness of sinful flesh' (Romans 8:3). He was among us in that nature which in every other instance is sinful. But he was not sinful. Human nature and sinful nature are not synonymous terms. Sin is not a necessary element in human nature. It is an intrusion. God created Adam without sin, and Eve too. They were fully human and only became sinners later. When Jesus came as the last Adam, he came with a human nature as real and as complete as that of the first Adam. But he was sinless and remained so. This does not only mean that he was able to avoid sinning, and that he did so; but it also means that it was impossible for him to sin because of the essential bond between his human and divine natures—a point we will come to shortly.

However, sinlessness in Jesus was not merely a neutral quality of innocence, as it was in the first Adam. The New Testament speaks of him sharing fully in all our experiences, and especially in the realm of temptation, which he always overcame. Temptation means nothing if it does not comprise striving against the lure of sin. It entails resisting its enticements. When we read that our Lord was 'in all points tempted as we are, yet without sin', we know that although the inducement to sin was real and powerful, it left him immaculate (Hebrews 4:15).

The sinlessness of Christ has frequently been denied in history and is still denied by various individuals and groups today. It is argued that there is an antecedent improbability of such a perfect life as that portrayed in the Gospels. Besides, it is said, how can we claim sinlessness for one whose life is virtually unknown before his thirtieth birthday? We point such objectors to Christ's deity, and rest our case on that fact. We remind them that those who lived closest to him, and were in the best position to know, confirmed his sinlessness. We point out that the three and a half years of his public ministry are consonant with the claim that he was sinless all through his life, but that they are meaningless if this claim is not admitted.

As our High Priest the Lord Jesus Christ is described as being 'holy, harmless, undefiled, separate from sinners' (Hebrews 7:26). This is an astonishing statement. Holiness is the moral quality of God, which renders him separate from his creatures. The other terms teach that Christ was guileless and unpolluted, free from all moral impurity and defilement, and not to be numbered with sinners, from whom he was obviously distinct.

Other plain statements tell us that 'in him there is no sin' (1 John 3:5), he 'committed no sin' (1 Peter 2:22) and that he 'knew no sin' (2 Corinthians 5:21). He was 'without blemish and without spot' (1 Peter 1:19). These statements were made by men who had lived in close intimacy with Christ for over three years and saw Jesus not only in public, but in what we call 'unguarded moments'. Not only so, but they were Jews whose minds were steeped in the Old Testament's teaching that Jehovah alone is without sin. They would not easily have attributed sinlessness to a fellow man. Their comments are all the more convincing in that they are made while they are writing about other subjects. They are asides. They are not out to labour the point. But their every thought of Christ's life was of a life lived out on this earth which was as holy and as morally pure as the life of God in heaven.

Made sin

It is true that on the cross God made Christ, judicially, 'to be sin' (2 Corinthians 5:21). But it is also true that he 'offered himself without spot to God' (Hebrews 9:14). Our sins were laid to his account when he died in our place. In his own life and character he was free from the depravity which all other men and women inherit from their parents. This, as we have seen, was because of the sanctifying power of the Holy Spirit, which ensured that nothing other than a 'holy one' was in Mary's womb, and born of her. He did not come into the world with a sinful nature, and he lived here without committing any actual sin. Our planet has witnessed the presence of a sinless man among universally sinful men and women!

Not even Christ's enemies (and he had plenty!) could convict him of any moral error. His challenge, 'Which of you convicts me of sin?' (John 8:46) met with no response. His enemies made frivolous charges from time to time, but when they finally brought him to trial their accusations had to be of a political nature and the witnesses had to be bribed. Not even hell itself was able to find any fault in Jesus of Nazareth. When the demons cried out in his presence, it was to testify that he was 'the Holy One of God' (Mark 1:24). At the time of his arrest Jesus was able to claim, 'The ruler of this world is coming, and he has nothing in me' (John 14:30).

Without sin

Jesus never made any confession of sin. Nor did he join with his disciples in praying, 'Forgive us our sins' (Luke 11:4). He never had the slightest sense of any moral discontent with himself. Although he had a keen moral judgement which could detect the slightest hypocrisy in others, he saw no fault in himself. He demanded penitence, but was never penitent. He never revealed the least consciousness that he had fallen short of his own exacting standards. Usually the more saintly a person becomes, the more troubled he becomes about his continuing imperfections. But not so Jesus. He was without sin. Because of this the Scriptures portray him as the one in whom the ideal man is realized (Hebrews 2:8–9; 1 Corinthians 15:45; 2 Corinthians 3:18; Philippians 3:21). Some students consider that his title 'the Son of Man', which we studied earlier, is a further indication that he answered to the perfect ideal of humanity.

But could Jesus have sinned? There has been a great deal of arguing on this point, not only in history but also again more recently. But there never should have been any argument at all. We must never forget that Jesus was and is the God-Man, in whom a divine and a human nature are indissolubly united. Although what is attributed to one nature cannot be attributed to the other nature, whatever is done in either nature can be attributed to the person who is our Lord Jesus Christ. If he could have sinned, then the Son of God could have sinned, which is unthinkable. We shall return later to this question of the relationship of the two natures to the one person.

Temptations

This does not mean that our Lord's temptations were unreal. A sea wall may resist the beatings of the storm for a while, but it gets washed away eventually. The granite cliffs, which cannot similarly be washed away, endure levels and strengths of pounding which no sea wall anywhere has ever experienced. Simply because our Lord could not sin, he endured an intensity of temptation unknown to, and never experienced by, any other member of the human race. The awfulness of this experience makes him one who can give us exactly the aid we need when we ourselves are tempted (Hebrews 4:14–16).

But there is another point. If Jesus could have sinned while on earth, he could sin now. Is he not 'the same yesterday, today, and for ever'? (Hebrews 13:8). Could our eternal salvation be built on so shaky a foundation?

The necessity of his manhood

And it *is* upon Christ's real but sinless humanity that our salvation is built.

It is man that has sinned, and it is man that must pay the penalty for sinning. Such a penalty involves the suffering of both body and soul, such as only a man is capable of bearing (now see again John 12:27; Acts 3:18; Hebrews 2:14; 9:22). And as such a penalty involves suffering also in this life, it was necessary that Christ should assume human nature, not only in its constituent parts, but also with all those weaknesses, limitations and infirmities to which it has been liable since the Fall. This is why Christ became subject to human limitations of knowledge, experienced hunger and thirst and knew sorrow and pain. In this way he descended to the depths of degradation to which mankind has fallen (Hebrews 2:17–18).

However, at the same time he had to be a sinless man. A man who was himself a sinner, and thus had to forfeit his own life, could never atone for others (Hebrews 7:26). Only a true human Mediator, who had personal experience of all the woes of mankind, and had never yielded to any temptation, could enter sympathetically into all the experiences, trials, difficulties and temptations of man. The Lord Jesus Christ is exactly such a Mediator (Hebrews 2:17–18; 4:15–5:2). Not only so, but he is also a perfect human example for us to follow (Matthew 11:29; John 13:13–17; Philippians 2:4–8; Hebrews 12:1–3; 1 Peter 1:21).

O Love, how deep, how broad, how high!
It fills the heart with ecstasy,
That God, the Son of God, should take
Our mortal form, for mortals' sake.

He sent no angel to our race,
Of higher or of lower place;
But wore the robe of human frame
Himself, and to this lost world came.

For us He was baptized and bore
His holy fast, and hungered sore;
For us temptation sharp He knew,
For us the tempter overthrew.

For us He prayed, for us He taught,
For us His daily works He wrought:
By words and signs and actions thus
Still seeking, not Himself, but us.

For us to wicked men betrayed,
Scourged, mocked, in purple robe arrayed,
He bore the shameful cross and death,
For us at length gave up His breath.

For us He rose from death again;
For us He went on high to reign;
For us He sent His Spirit here
To guide, to strengthen and to cheer.

To Him whose boundless love has won
Salvation for us through His Son,
To God the Father, glory be,
Both now and through eternity.

Anonymous hymn from a fifteenth-century manuscript, translated by Benjamin Webb (1820–1885), who also added the doxology.

6

A man now and for ever

We have seen that the Scriptures of the Old Testament promised that the eternal Son of God would come among us as a man; and we have seen that he did so. But we must never think that the Lord Jesus Christ was a man only during the few years that he walked this earth, and that he ceased to be one at his resurrection, or when he ascended into heaven. He is *still* a man. And he will be one for ever.

A man resurrected

It was as a man that he rose from the dead: 'For since by man came death, by man also came the resurrection of the dead' (1 Corinthians 15:21). The resurrection is a mystery, and the actual nature of the resurrection body is beyond the scope of human knowledge (1 Corinthians 15:35-44). Nevertheless, the New Testament insists that the resurrection body of our Lord was not only real, but was the same body which had been entombed. This was exactly what Christ himself had previously predicted (John 2:19-21). Throughout the New Testament his resurrection is appealed to as a miraculous attestation of the truth of his mission, but unless his body rose literally from the dead there was nothing miraculous about his continued life.

The whole language of the inspired narratives is geared to

underline the truth that the man who died was alive again, in the very same body that he had before. The rolling away of the stone, the empty grave-clothes and other details all necessarily imply this. The fact that he did not rise until the third day serves to emphasize that the resurrection was something physical, and not a mere continuance of a spiritual experience. We also read how his body was seen, handled and examined for a period of forty days, so that the fact of his physical resurrection could be seen to be indisputable. He was seen not only at dawn or at dusk, but repeatedly in the clear light of day. His body was visible and tangible, the very same one as he had had before.

A physical resurrection

Jesus himself challenged the impression that his resurrection body was purely spiritual. We read in Luke 24:37–43 that the disciples 'were terrified and frightened, and supposed they had seen a spirit. And he said to them, "Why are you troubled? And why do doubts arise in your hearts? Behold my hands and my feet, that it is I myself. Handle me and see, for a spirit does not have flesh and bones as you see I have." When he had said this, he showed them his hands and his feet. But while they still did not believe for joy, and marvelled, he said to them, "Have you any food here?" So they gave him a piece of a broiled fish and some honeycomb. And he took it and ate in their presence.' From what we know of the resurrection body, there was no need for Jesus to have eaten this food. The purpose was evidently to satisfy fully the doubting and enquiring disciples that he was as much a physical man after his resurrection as he had been before.

The final proof that our Lord's resurrection body was the same one as had died lies in the fact that it bore the marks of his crucifixion (John 20:27). And yet it possessed certain characteristics which are not true of our bodies, and which were not true of his before his death. It had new properties. For example, the narratives seem to suggest that our Lord passed through the swathing encumbrance of his grave-clothes, and through the rock-hewn tomb (John 20:5–8; Matthew 28:1–2). The rolling away of the stone took place *after* the Lord had left his tomb! Its purpose was not to let the Lord out, but to let the disciples in! Our Lord certainly also passed through locked doors to visit his disciples (John 20:19,26). His body had obviously undergone a remarkable change so that although he was usually easily recognized, he could become unrecognizable at will; and he could also suddenly appear and disappear in a surprising manner (Luke 24:31,36; John 20:13; 21:4,12).

The same, yet different

How can we say that our Lord rose in the same body in which he had died, and yet also say that that body was different? The answer is that the resurrection of Christ did not consist in his mere coming to life again. It was not simply a reuniting of his human body and human spirit. If this were all that it involved, he could not be called 'the firstfruits of those who have fallen asleep' (1 Corinthians 15:20), nor 'the firstborn from the dead' (Colossians 1:18; Revelation 1:5), since many others had been restored to life before him. Christ merits these titles because in him human nature, both body and soul, was restored to its original strength and perfection, and even raised to a higher level. His resurrection body, although in no way immaterial or ethereal, was also capable of moving naturally in the heavenly and invisible dimension of the spiritual world. It was a perfect instrument of the spirit. Although still fully a man, our Lord was no longer bound to the conditions of his previous humiliation. The heavenly life, invisible to human eyes, with a body adapted to this condition, was the normal experience of our Lord after his resurrection. His appearances were a gracious condescension for our sake, to convince us utterly that the very same man who had died was now alive for evermore still a man, but capable both in body and spirit of moving in a more exalted dimension. He was no longer earth-bound. He thus showed what is to be the final condition of redeemed mankind, and how different this condition is to be from the denuding of the body which was taught by Greek philosophy. In eternity we shall not be disembodied spirits, but will have glorified bodies!

A man ascended

For forty days after his resurrection our Lord continued to present his disciples with incontrovertible evidence that he was alive. 'He also presented himself alive after his suffering by many infallible proofs, being seen by them during forty days' (Acts 1:3). They had been 'slow of heart to believe' (Luke 24:25), and were not easily convinced that he whom they now saw alive was the very same Christ who had died. But for nearly six weeks they received the strongest possible proof, which so completely convinced them that none of them ever doubted the fact again. Their courageous testimony to the resurrection eventually cost most of them their lives, but they could not deny what they had seen and experienced. The man who had lived and died was alive again!

It was this man that they saw leave this earth in a manner entirely in keeping with the miraculous achievements of his life and work. The man who had died was the one who had risen; and the one who was risen was the one who ascended. His final departure was not a mere vanishing out of their sight, as it had been at Emmaus. Had it been so, they would have been uncertain as to whether or not he might reappear. This time, 'While they watched, he was taken up, and a cloud received him out of their sight … They looked steadfastly towards heaven as he went up …' (Acts 1:9–10).

It was not necessary for our Lord to go 'up' to return to his Father, but he chose this method of departure to convince them that they must not expect him to appear again. The event was real and objective, but it was also symbolic. No other mode of departure would have left the right impression. He was returning to the heaven from which he had come. But he was returning there as a man!

A resurrected human Lord had communed with them for forty days. It was this Lord who now ascended before their eyes. Everything about the event was calculated to assure them that he was as human in his ascension as he was before it. A human voice rang in their ears, giving them his final teaching. Human hands were outstretched to bless them (Luke 24:50). A human body ascended from the spot to which he had so recently led them. As they gazed at the sky, where a cloud received him out of their sight, two angels appeared, speaking of their departed and now invisible Lord by his human name (Acts 1:11). They were told that the Lord who would one day return would be no different from the one who had just left them. Every one of them left the Mount of Olives knowing that there was a man in heaven.

The ascension was a visible ascent of the person of the Mediator, according to his human nature, from earth to heaven. 'Jesus of Nazareth, a man …' is 'exalted to the right hand of God' (Acts 2:22,33). It was a local transition, a going from one place to another. But we must point out that the ascension also included a further change in the human nature of Christ, just as his resurrection had done before it. That event had not made him less human, and nor did this one. But now his human nature passed into the fulness of heavenly glory, and was perfectly adapted to the life of heaven. He is the same Jesus. He is just as much a man as before. But he is now glorified to the highest degree. The glory which he had had on earth was not at all the glory which he had had with the Father before the world existed. It was to this which he now, as a man, returned, 'far above all principality and power and might and dominion, and every name that is named, not only in this age but also in that which is to come' (Ephesians 1:21).

Our great High Priest

The believer loves to meditate on the exaltation of the Lord Jesus Christ. When he was among us he told his enemies, 'Hereafter you will see the Son of Man sitting at the right hand of the power'

(Matthew 26:64). It is wonderful to know that he who spoke these words is now in that glorious position! This is how both Stephen and Paul saw him (Acts 7:56; 9:4-6). This is how the apostles rejoiced to preach him (Acts 2:33-36; 5:31). This is how the epistles constantly present him (Romans 14:9; Philippians 2:9; Hebrews 2:7-8; 1 Peter 3:22). This is how he is seen in the closing book of God's book (Revelation 3:21; 22:1). The man who had descended to the lowest place of all, 'This man, after he had offered one sacrifice for sins for ever, sat down at the right hand of God' (Hebrews 10:12).

The expression 'right hand of God' is obviously not to be taken literally, but is a way of making it easier for our poor minds to grasp a profound truth. The expression, used in this way, undoubtedly comes from Psalm 110:1: 'Sit at my right hand, till I make your enemies your footstool.' To be seated at the right hand of a king was a mark of honour (1 Kings 2:19), but more seems to be suggested when this phrase is used of Christ. It means that Christ as Mediator rules on his Father's behalf over the universe and over the church. He has always done this as the eternal Son of God, but at his ascension he was publicly inaugurated into this position as *a man*, or, more accurately, as the God-Man.

The work of Christ

Christ's sitting 'at the right hand of God' does not, then, indicate that the life to which the risen Lord has ascended is a life of rest. We must not think of him as merely a passive recipient of divine dominion and power, majesty and glory, but as one who is actively engaged in the mediatorial work put into his hands by his Father.

This book is not about the work of Christ, but his person. However, it is important for us to note that he could not possibly do the work which he is now doing if he was not who he is. This is particularly true of his present high-priestly ministry. If the Lord Jesus Christ was not still a man, he could not be our great High Priest.

When we say that Christ is our High Priest, we mean that he is continually presenting his completed sacrifice to the Father as the sufficient basis for the bestowal of God's pardon to sinners, as the basis for our continued acceptance at God's throne and as the reason why our prayers should be heard and our service regarded with favour. Christ could not speak to God for us in this way, if he were not a man. The truth which brings us daily comfort is that 'There is one God and one Mediator between God and men, the *man* Christ Jesus' (1 Timothy 2:5, emphasis mine).

Our mediator

How could our Mediator guarantee our acceptance with God if he were not God himself? And how could he truly represent us to God if he were not also a man? This last point is not just a matter of simple logic. It is a divine requirement that whoever speaks to God on behalf of men should be 'taken from among men' (Hebrews 5:1, see Exodus 28:9,12,21,29). He must be linked to those whom he represents by the ties of a common humanity. In no other way would he be able to 'have compassion on those who are ignorant and going astray' (Hebrews 5:2). Although free from the sin which besets all other human priests, the Scriptures rejoice that this essential qualification for the high-priesthood is one which the Lord Jesus Christ meets (Hebrews 5:1-9). The whole theology of the high-priestly ministry of Christ, as found in the Epistle to the Hebrews, is built on the foundation that Christ is still a man.

When we are tempted, he is able to support and help us, because he knows exactly what we are going through. He understands our human feelings and he sympathizes with our weaknesses because there is no experience in our lives through which he has not already passed himself—with the single exception of yielding to the temptation to sin. He is able to deal with us tenderly and to give us exactly the help that we need (Hebrews 2:14-17; 4:14-16). His sympathy does not rest on the fact that he merely remembers what it is like to be a man. He is still a man himself, 'Jesus Christ ... the same yesterday, today, and for ever (Hebrews 13:8)—the man, once dead, who 'ever lives to make intercession for [us]' (Hebrews 7:25).

> Though now ascended up on high,
> He bends on earth a brother's eye;
> Partaker of the human name,
> He knows the frailty of our frame.
>
> Our fellow-sufferer yet retains
> A fellow-feeling of our pains,
> And still remembers in the skies
> His tears, his agonies and cries.
>
> In every pang that rends the heart
> The Man of sorrows has a part;
> He sympathizes with our grief,
> And to the sufferer sends relief.
>
> With boldness, therefore, at the throne,
> Let us make all our sorrows known;
> And ask the aid of heavenly power
> To help us in the evil hour.
>
> Scottish Paraphrases, 1781.

A man at his advent

In heaven, invisible to our eyes, the man Christ Jesus pursues his high-priestly work. But he will not always be invisible. At last God will 'send Jesus Christ, who was preached to you before, whom heaven must receive until the times of restoration of all things, which God has spoken by the mouth of all his holy prophets since the world began' (Acts 3:20–21). Then 'the Lord Jesus [will be] revealed from heaven with his mighty angels' (2 Thessalonians 1:7). 'Behold, he is coming with clouds, and every eye will see him, and they also who pierced him. And all the tribes of the earth will mourn because of him. Even so, Amen' (Revelation 1:7).

In like manner

The Second Coming of Christ will be infinitely greater in glory than his ascension. Only a small number of people saw that event, but the whole of humanity will witness his return. There were but two angels that day on Olivet, but next time every angel in heaven will attend him. None the less, the return of Christ will be an exact reversal of his ascension. Instead of going up, 'The Lord himself will descend from heaven' (1 Thessalonians 4:16). Instead of a cloud receiving him from sight, 'as the lightning comes from the east and flashes to the west, so also will the coming of the Son of Man be' (Matthew 24:27). The advent will be a perfect fulfilment of the angelic promise: 'This same Jesus, who was taken up from you into heaven, will so come in like manner as you saw him go into heaven' (Acts 1:11).

This same Jesus! The Lord himself! It is clear that the advent will be the coming of the very same person who ascended almost two thousand years ago. The God-Man who promised, 'I will come' and 'I am coming quickly!' (John 14:3; Revelation 22:7) will keep his word. At his ascension the angels were at pains to use his human name when speaking of his return, as was Paul in 2 Thessalonians 1:7, quoted above. It is true that his advent is 'the day of God' (2 Peter 3:12). But it is also 'the coming of the Son of Man' (Matthew 24:37). It was as a man that he left us. It is as a man that he is seated at God's right hand. It is as a man that the unchangeable Christ will return.

This point is underlined by the New Testament's insistence that his coming will be both physical and visible. In speaking of that momentous event it mentions 'his glorious body' (Philippians 3:21), his 'shout' (1 Thessalonians 4:16) and reminds us that 'we shall see him as he is' (1 John 3:2). It is the day when he shall 'appear' (Colossians 3:4; Hebrews 9:28). Who can tell what a 'glorious appearing' (Titus 2:13) it will be when 'the Lord Jesus [will be] revealed' (2 Thessalonians 1:7) and 'every eye will see him'? (Revelation 1:7). The New Testament knows nothing of a merely spiritual coming, or one that will be invisible. The Lord Jesus Christ who left us will visibly return to earth in a body.

The resurrection of the dead

Immediately after his return our Lord will fulfil the promise made in John 5:28-29: 'Do not marvel at this; for the hour is coming in which all who are in the graves will hear his voice and come forth—those who have done good, to the resurrection of life, and those who have done evil, to the resurrection of condemnation.' This work of resurrecting the human race gives further proof of Christ's continuing humanity. The New Testament reveals that although we will be raised in the very bodies in which we have died, these bodies will be changed (1 Corinthians 15:51-52; Philippians 3:21). Because believers' bodies are members of Christ, and belong to him, their resurrection will be analogous to his. What this meant for him we have already studied. He 'will transform our lowly body that it may be conformed to his glorious body, according to the working by which he is able even to subdue all things to himself' (Philippians 3:21). These words would be meaningless if, at the resurrection, our risen Lord was not still a man himself in his own resurrection body.

After this, we are told, both resurrected believers and those believers who are still alive at the Lord's return 'shall be caught up together … in the clouds to meet the Lord in the air' (1 Thessalonians 4:17). There will be a physical gathering of Christian people to their Lord. He himself will not be in all places, but to gather physically with him it will be necessary for all his people to go to the same place. What else can this mean but that he still has a human nature, and in that nature can only be present in one place at a time? Our Lord will still be a man, even on the Last Day.

Judgement

It is a man who, after the resurrection, will judge the world. The gathering of all nations and the separating of humanity, as a shepherd divides his sheep from the goats, is a work of 'the Son of Man' (Matthew 25:31-32). That man will be exactly the same one whom God raised from the dead, 'Because he has appointed a day on which he will judge the world in righteousness by the man whom he has ordained. He has given assurance of this to all by raising him from the dead' (Acts 17:31; see John 5:22; Acts 10:42; 2 Timothy 4:1). This honour of being the Judge belongs intrinsically to Christ as God, but was conferred on him as a man in reward for his obedience, even to the cross, and as a part of his exaltation (John 5:27; Philippians 2:9-10). This also is a mystery which we can but state, for it is beyond our comprehension. The exaltation of the man Christ Jesus will reach its climax on the Last Day, when to the one carrying the human name of 'Jesus' every knee shall bow, and every tongue shall confess that he is Lord (Philippians 2:10-11).

The Lord Jesus Christ will never cease to be a man. When he took upon himself our human nature in the womb of the virgin Mary, he did so for ever. He could never lay aside his humanity without dissociating himself from his human name of Jesus and without ceasing to be the Son of Man. Since his resurrection he is no longer subject, as we still are, to the natural limitations of life on earth. But he does not cease to have the essential attributes of humanity. If we could but draw back the veil a little and could gaze into the heavenly dimension, we should have to cry with dying Stephen, 'Look! I see the heavens opened and the Son of Man standing at the right hand of God!' (Acts 7:56). And that is how it will always be.

> And didst Thou love the race that loved not Thee?
> And didst Thou take to heaven a human brow?
> Dost plead with man's voice by the marvellous sea?
> Art Thou his kinsman now?
>
> O God, O Kinsman, loved, but not enough!
> Man, with eyes majestic after death!

Whose feet have toiled along our pathways rough,
Whose lips drawn human breath!

By that one likeness which is ours and Thine,
By that one nature which doth hold us kin,
By that high heaven where, sinless,
Thou dost shine, To draw us sinners in;

By Thy last silence in the judgement hall,
By long foreknowledge of the deadly tree,
By darkness, by the wormwood and the gall,
O pray Thee, visit me.

Come, lest this heart should, cold and cast away,
Die ere the Guest adored she entertain—
Lest eyes that never saw Thine earthly day
Should miss Thy heavenly reign.

Jean Ingelow,
1820–1897.

Christ—his unipersonality

7

One person

We have seen that the Lord Jesus Christ is truly God. He is also truly man, having supernaturally become one of the human race, without sin. In this chapter we are going to see that he is yet but one person.

The Council of Chalcedon

A good starting-point for this subject is to mention the ancient ecclesiastical Council of Chalcedon. During the first two centuries of the Christian church it was their faith as a whole that Christian men and women were called upon to defend against all-out pagan opposition. During the third and fourth centuries the attack became less generalized, and Satan concentrated his efforts on seeking to destroy the doctrine of the Trinity. But no sooner had the church survived these attacks than there began an attack upon the doctrine of the person of Christ. We shall consider some of the heresies that arose in this period in chapter 9. Suffice it to say at this point that in the light of these attacks the church defined the true doctrine of Christ's person at the Council of Chalcedon in AD 451. A period of over a century had witnessed almost every conceivable method of interpreting the biblical data. But at last a formula was framed which successfully guarded from destructive misconceptions the essential teaching which God's Word supplies.

The principal part of Chalcedon's 'Definition of Faith' can be found in Appendix 1 of this book, but we may notice here that its definition focused upon the fact that in Christ 'two whole, perfect, and distinct natures, the Godhead and the manhood, were inseparably joined together in one person; without conversion, composition, or confusion', as the Westminster Confession of 1646 was later to summarize Chalcedon's statement. Chalcedon was anxious to acknowledge what we have discovered from our own studies in the Scriptures, as presented in this book so far. Our Lord Jesus Christ has two natures. But he is not two people: 'The peculiar properties of each nature being preserved, and concurring to one person and one substance, not parted or divided into two persons, but one and the same Son, and only begotten, God the Word, the Lord Jesus Christ.'

Chalcedon's formula was mainly negative. This should not surprise us, because the purpose of the council was to defend the church against heretical views. In systematic form, it clearly stated what the Scriptures teach regarding the person of Christ, but made no attempt to explain the mystery. This was just as well, because the mystery is not capable of natural explanation. The council simply stated what the Bible teaches, but what no human mind has ever been able to grasp. The Lord Jesus Christ is God and man in one person.

Set forth in Chalcedon's statement is the great truth that the eternal Son of God took upon himself our humanity, and the impression is never given that the man Jesus acquired divinity. Centuries have gone by, and new doctrinal statements in the forms of creeds, confessions and catechisms have been drawn up, used and forgotten. But the church has never really progressed beyond Chalcedon. The formula drawn up in just three weeks in October 451 remains the best statement on the subject. For ourselves, we need to satisfy ourselves as to whether its statement is a true expression of the teaching of the Scriptures, or whether it is nothing more than the man-made theology of 630 ancient bishops.

Some terms defined

We will not get very far in understanding what Chalcedon was saying unless we clearly understand the difference between the terms 'nature' and 'person'.

When we put together all the essential qualities of a thing — the qualities which make it that thing—we have its 'nature'. Human nature requires that we have a true body, physically composed of the requisite chemicals, and arranged to form the organs which make up the whole. In addition there must be the God-given invisible side of our nature which animates the whole, and which we call 'a reasonable soul'. As we have seen, Christ had such a nature, and still does so. He also has a divine nature. This means that he has all the divine attributes in one indivisible essence. In other words, he is not composed of eternity, unchangeableness, holiness, etc., all added together—but all of him is eternal, all of him is unchangeable, all of him is holy, etc. Whatever is essential to man's existence as man, and God's existence as God, our Lord Jesus Christ had, and has. This is what we mean when we refer to his two 'natures'.

By 'person' we mean that the nature has something added which gives it individuality. As fellow humans we have the same chemical structure, and bodies which are different from each other only in minor features. Our organs are the same, differing only in size and shape. But one human is not another. The real 'you' of each one is different. Each human has individual subsistence. He is not just a collection of essential qualities, but is able to reason and is the responsible subject of his own actions. Chalcedon's formula teaches that although Jesus has whatever is essential to God's existence as God, and to man's existence as man, there was only one Jesus. There were not two real 'you's in the God-Man. Christ's divine nature had an independent existence from all eternity, up until the moment when the 'holy one' was conceived in Mary's womb; and the person possessed of that divine nature was the eternal Son of God.

However, his human nature never had an independent existence, but from its beginning was in mysterious and permanent union with his divine nature. This means that the 'real you' of the God-Man was the same 'real you' as the eternal Son of God before his incarnation. He acquired an additional nature in Mary's womb, but continued to be the person that he always was. The incarnation was a conjunction, in one person, of all that belongs to Godhead and all that belongs to manhood. We state it again—the Lord Jesus Christ is God and man in one person.

Closer definition

Let us state all this more precisely, so that there can be no misunderstanding. The Lord Jesus Christ is but one person. The person that he is now is the person that he always was—the unchangeable Word, the eternal Son of God. But it is not correct to say that the person of our Saviour is divine only. The incarnation constituted him a complex person, possessed of two natures. He is the God-Man.

The fact that the Lord Jesus Christ has a human nature does not make him a human person. The eternal Word did not take over a human personality, so that there are two persons in Christ. He simply assumed a human nature. At the very point where we have a sinful person, he has the person of the eternal Word.

On the other hand, it is not correct to say, as do so many otherwise reliable theological books, that the human nature of Christ is impersonal. They speak of the true body and soul of Jesus of Nazareth, but do not admit that there was a real human 'you' expressing himself through them. Because of its extreme importance, we underline the point made previously. Christ's human nature never had any independent subsistence of its own. But this does not mean that it was devoid of a human 'you'. It simply means that the human 'you', from its very inception, was in perfect union with the 'you' of the eternal Son of God. It has never existed apart from him and, if we may put it like this for the moment, was absorbed into him from the very commencement of its existence. As Louis Berkhof puts it, with some obvious dependence on Leontius of Byzantium: 'Strictly speaking, however, the human nature of Christ was not for a moment impersonal. The Logos assumed that nature into personal subsistence with Himself. The human nature has its personal existence in the person of the Logos. It is in-personal rather than impersonal.'[1]

We insist therefore that the human nature of Christ was in no way imperfect or incomplete. No essential quality necessary for man's existence as man was missing. That nature found its individuality and personal subsistence in the person of the eternal Son of God. That does not mean, of course, that Christ had no human consciousness and no human will. Consciousness and will are attributes which belong to that list of essential qualities which make up human nature. Christ could not have existed as man without them. His possession of a complete human nature means that he was in possession of these two features too.

If all this sounds unduly complicated, at least let this final paragraph of this section be pondered until it is grasped. We are saying that a divine person, who possessed a divine nature from eternity, assumed a human nature, and now has both. He remains exactly the person he has always been, while the two natures he possesses are entirely separate, distinct, unchanged and complete.

Biblical proof

This teaching of the two natures in one person is difficult enough for the human mind to state, and certainly far too high for our limited (and now fallen) minds to comprehend. We are discussing a reality beyond the scope of our understanding, for which there is no analogy. We accept it, not on the ground that we have grasped or mastered it, but because the evident teaching of God's Word moves us to do so. No one can come to believe this truth who is not willing to submit to what God himself has revealed. But how precisely does the Bible present this doctrine to us?

It does so by three strands of teaching. The first is its entire failure to give us any evidence of two personalities in our Lord Jesus Christ. If there had been a dual personality in our Saviour, we would naturally expect to see indications of it in the Scriptures. Such indications are completely lacking. In all that is recorded of our Lord Jesus Christ there is no word spoken by him, no action performed and no attribute predicated of him, which suggests that he is not one single indivisible person. Although he was conscious of being divine, and of being human, there is not the slightest trace anywhere of dual personality. He had two centres of consciousness, but only one of self-consciousness. This is a fact of considerable importance.

In the Bible we sometimes find the persons of the Trinity speaking to each other as 'you', and of each other as 'him', 'he' etc. But there is no such distinction of personalities in the inner life of the Lord Jesus Christ. There is no interchange of 'I' and 'you' between his two natures. The personal pronouns are always used by him as if he were a single person. Moreover, Jesus never uses the plural of himself, as God does, for instance, in Genesis 1:26; 3:22 and 11:7. If there is any exception to this it can only be at John 3:11, but it is more likely that the 'we' of this verse refers to Jesus and those associated with him, over against Nicodemus and his group. The fact is unassailable. Jesus did not think of himself as a 'we' or an 'us', but only as an 'I' and a 'me'. Clearly possessed of two natures, there was nevertheless only one Christ.

A second line of biblical evidence is found in considering the terms in which the New Testament writers wrote of Christ. As he thought of himself, so did the apostles think of him too. Passage after passage refers to both natures of Christ, but makes it perfectly plain that only one person is in mind. So in

Romans 1:3-4 Paul speaks of Christ as 'born of the seed of David according to the flesh, and declared to be the Son of God ...' But who is this who has two natures? Is he one person or two? Paul answers definitely by saying that he is writing concerning 'his Son Jesus Christ our Lord'.

Another typical example is Galatians 4:4-5, where Paul writes that 'God sent forth his Son, born of a woman ...' There is not a hint that two personalities came to redeem them that were under the law, but one. Both natures are represented as united in one person. Those who would like a further sample of the same thing should ponder Philippians 2:5-11, or any other passage which refers to the two natures of the Saviour. They will find that the picture is everywhere consistent. The Bible speaks unfailingly of one 'who although he is God and man, is not two but one Christ' (Athanasian Creed).

This does not mean that the Bible teaches that divinity in the abstract was simply manifested in human nature. It was not some ethereal, impossible-to-pin-down influence which united itself to man. No, indeed. At this point the picture is equally consistent. A divine person, the second person of the blessed Trinity, the eternal Son of God himself, assumed human nature. The eternal Word 'became flesh' (John 1:1-2,14). The one who came in our likeness, in human flesh, was God's 'own Son', 'the eternally blessed God' (Romans 8:3; 9:5; see 1 Timothy 3:16; Hebrews 2:11-14; 1 John 4:2-3).

The God-Man

But there is a third line of scriptural proof which settles the issue beyond question. It is so clear that no heretic, however devious, is capable of wresting it to serve his own ends. It is the fact that what can be true of only one or the other of Christ's two natures is attributed, not to the nature, but to the one person. He is spoken of in terms true of either one or the other of his natures. Again and again the attributes of one nature are predicated of the person, while that person is spoken of by a title only fitting for someone who has the other nature. Here is conclusive proof that he who has two natures is but one person.

Some examples

The previous paragraph may well be perplexing for anyone who is studying this glorious subject for the first time, so let us give some examples. In several New Testament texts human attributes and actions are reckoned to be those of a person who is given divine titles. He is spoken of by a title proper to his divine nature, while the action attributed to him is proper to his human nature. A classic example is Acts 20:28, where Paul speaks of 'the church of God which he purchased with his own blood'. Only creatures can shed blood, while God, who is a Spirit, cannot. Christ was able to shed blood only by virtue of his human nature. But who was this Christ who thus redeemed the church? Was he merely a human Christ? No, he is 'God'. What could only be true of his human nature is said to have been accomplished by the divine person. There is not a human Christ and a divine Christ—two Christs. There is but one Christ. Because he is one person, with two natures, we may speak of him as God and of him as the one who shed redeeming blood.

In just the same way 1 Corinthians 2:8 speaks of a 'crucified … Lord of glory', and Colossians 1:13–14 of 'the Son of his love, in whom we have redemption through his blood'. Can a divine nature be crucified? Can it shed blood? These things can be true only of his human nature. It was, none the less, a divine person who is said to have redeemed us. It was none other than 'the Lord of glory'. Our salvation has not been accomplished by a human Christ who is separate and distinct from the divine Christ. What could be done only by a man is attributed to God's eternal Son. What he did by virtue of one nature is not attributed to the other nature, but to the person who is possessed of both natures. Two natures he certainly had, and has. But there is only one Christ.

Other New Testament texts give us exactly the same

phenomenon, but the other way round. Divine attributes and actions are reckoned to be those of a person who has human titles. He is spoken of by a title proper to his human nature, while the action attributed to him is proper only to his divine nature. What can be done only by one who is divine is specifically said to be done by one whose humanity is emphasized. So in John 3:13 Jesus speaks of himself as someone who 'came down from heaven', but stresses that he who did this is a man, 'the Son of Man'. What no man can do, he, who is a man, has done! This is not because he had a human nature before he came to earth. It is because he who conversed as a man with Nicodemus was the same person as had come from above. He came down from heaven by virtue of his divine nature, but sat and talked that night in Jerusalem by virtue of his human nature. But he was the same person. This is why Christ could later pose the question: 'What then if you should see the Son of Man ascend where he was before?' (John 6:62). The assuming of a human nature in addition to his divine nature had not altered the real 'you' who Jesus was.

All of this is only possible because Christ, constituted of two natures, is one person. He may therefore be called by either divine or human titles, and both divine and human attributes and actions may be reckoned to be his. He is still God when he dies, and still man when he raises people from their graves.

Whatever Christ does as Mediator, he does by virtue of both his natures. We must always remember, however, that while the person is one, the natures remain entirely distinct. This is a point to which we will return in our next chapter. Whatever is done in either nature is the action of the person that Christ is. But what can be done only by virtue of his possessing one nature must never be reckoned to the other nature. Scripture never does this, and nor must we. Human attributes and actions are never ascribed to Christ's divine nature, nor are divine attributes and actions ever ascribed to his human nature. But both are ascribed to the one Christ.

The unity of Christ's person

The more we study the Gospels, the less inclined are we to say that our Lord did any particular action by virtue of his being God, or another action by virtue of his being man. We do not see him sometimes as God, and at other times as man. What strikes us is the unity of his person. Before long we can only think of him for what he is—the God-Man, who acted in all things as a single person.

John Chrysostom (c.345–407) wrote an eloquent paragraph on this subject: 'I do not think of Christ as God alone, or man alone, but both together. For I know he was hungry, and I know that with five loaves he fed five thousand. I know he was thirsty, and I know that he turned the water into wine. I know he was carried in a ship, and I know that he walked on the sea. I know that he died, and I know that he raised the dead. I know he was set before Pilate, and I know that he sits with the Father on his throne. I know that he was worshipped by angels, and I know that he was stoned by the Jews. And truly some of these I ascribe to the human and others to the divine nature. For by reason of this he is said to have been both God and Man.'

The personality of Christ is that of the eternal Son of God who, in time, took a human soul and body into personal union with himself. This remarkable person did not begin to exist, and therefore was not constituted in the womb of the virgin Mary. 'Before Abraham was, *I am*', he could say (John 8:58, emphasis mine). Although in the flesh, he is 'the eternally blessed God' (Romans 9:5). The person of Christ is eternal, and not formed in time. But in time this eternal and divine person took a human nature, and a human personality into his personality. Just as the body, with its wonderful constitution of organs, nerves, senses and passions etc., grows in the womb into the personality of the soul, so the human nature of Christ, from the instant of its conception, grew into the eternal personality of the Son of God. There are in Christ, therefore, two natures but one person.

There is a human as well as a divine nature but the personality is that of the eternal Son of God. His humanity began to exist in Mary's womb, but his person existed from eternity. His divinity is personal, his humanity is in-personal and his divine nature and his human nature one person.

> God of God,
> Light of Light,
> Lo, He abhors not the virgin's womb;
> Very God, Begotten, not created:
>
> O come, let us adore Him,
> O come, let us adore Him,
> O come, let us adore Him,
> Christ the Lord!
>
> From a Latin hymn,
> translated by Frederick Oakeley (1802–1880) and others.

Endnote

1 Berkhof, *Systematic Theology* (Banner of Truth Trust), p. 322.

8

Two distinct natures

The divine and human natures in Christ are not mixed or confused in any way, but remain two pure and distinct natures, constituting one person for ever. This is the truth that we come to in this chapter.

Self-evident

Our human minds cannot understand or explain how *two* self-conscious intelligences, how *two* self-determined free agents, can constitute one person. Yet this is exactly what the sacred Scriptures reveal concerning our Lord Jesus Christ.

In order to simplify the matter, and to evade some of its difficulties, some people have supposed that in the person of Christ there was no human soul, but that his divine spirit took the place of the human soul in his human body. Others have so far separated his two natures as to make him two persons—a God and a man intimately united. Others have felt that the incarnation must of necessity have caused a change in at least one of the natures, so that either the divine nature was reduced and humanized (so that he was no longer the same in substance as the Father and the Holy Spirit, and no longer equal to them); or that the human nature was greatly exalted, indeed deified, by being united to his divine nature (so that he was no longer truly 'one of us'). But what is of particular importance for this chapter is that others have so pressed the two natures together that they have come to believe that our Lord had neither *a* divine nor a human nature, but a *third* nature resulting from the mixing of both—a nature which was somehow midway between the two.

Most of these points have already been answered in this book. We have seen that Christ had a true human soul, as well as a human body. We have seen that although he is both God and man, he is but one single person. Our studies have also convinced us of the integrity of both his natures. There was nothing in our first three chapters to lead us to believe that his divine nature was in any way reduced. There was nothing in chapters 4 to 6 to indicate that his humanity gave him anything less than full identification with our race. The truth that Christ's two natures remain separate and unconfused is, to any serious student of the Scriptures, self-evident. The divine did not permeate the human, nor was the human absorbed by the divine. Leo the Great (died 461) put it this way: 'He ... combined both natures in a league so close that the lower was not consumed by receiving glory, nor the higher lessened by assuming lowliness.'

We have seen repeatedly that Christ always continued to be true God, and is now also a true man. There is not a hint anywhere that he is something between the two. It must be plain that the essential properties of divinity cannot be communicated to humanity. How can a *man* be made to be infinite, self-existent and eternal? If he could, he would cease to *be* man! In addition, not even God can create deity. Because deity is eternal and self-existent, it is, by definition, uncreatable. No humanity can be made divine.

Humanity cannot absorb divinity, and divinity cannot absorb humanity. If Christ's deity had taken on the limitations of humanity, it would have ceased to have been deity! But no deity can ever cease to exist. It is, by definition, self-existent, unchangeable and eternal.

Hence since Christ is, as we have seen, both God and man,

it follows that he cannot be a mixture of both, because such a mixture is *neither*. We say it once more—once it is acknowledged that he has both natures, it follows *as a self-evident truth* that he has them 'without mixture, without change, without division, without separation; the diversity of the two natures not being at all destroyed by their union, but the peculiar properties of each nature being preserved' (Chalcedon). How could the divine nature have remained truly and completely divine, and the human nature fully human, if the two natures had not remained *entirely* distinct, 'without conversion, composition, or confusion? (*Westminster Confession*).

Effect on his divine nature

The union of the divine and human natures in the single person of the Lord Jesus Christ is usually referred to as 'the hypostatical union'. The fact that this union did not alter either nature in any way, or make them less than distinct, does not mean that they were unaffected by the union. His divine nature, being a divine nature, was of course eternal, immutable and incapable of addition, and therefore remained essentially unchanged. The whole immutable divine essence continued to exist as the person of the eternal Word, but now embraced a perfect human nature in the unity of his person. That human nature became the instrument of his will. In this way the *relation* of the divine nature to creation changed, although the nature itself remained unaltered. The eternal Son of God was now 'God with us' (Matthew 1:23), God 'manifested in the flesh' (1 Timothy 3:16).

Of course, the divine nature of Christ remained incapable of suffering and death, free from ignorance, and unsusceptible to weakness and temptation. It was not a *divine nature* which had assumed flesh, but the Son of God as *person* who had become incarnate. *He* could be ignorant and weak, and could suffer and die. This was because he had assumed an additional nature capable of these things, and not because there had been any change in his divine nature.

We must be clear that the properties of both the human and the divine natures of Christ are the properties of the person that he is. The person can be said to be almighty, omniscient, omnipresent, and so on. He can also be called a man of sorrows, of limited knowledge and power, and subject to human want and miseries. But we must be careful to guard against thinking that anything belonging to his divine nature was communicated or transferred to the human nature, or vice versa. Christ shared in human weaknesses, although the Deity cannot. Christ participates in the essential perfections of the Godhead, although humanity cannot. This is possible because he is one person, the God-Man. We do not have to postulate any change in either of his natures, although we are admitting that their union did not leave them unaffected.

Effect on his human nature

The human nature of Christ, from the very first moment of its existence, enjoyed the glory of being united to the divine and eternal Word. It never had any existence apart from him, and therefore was exalted from its very inception in a way no other human nature has been exalted before or since. Inevitably it was perfect, being one constituent of the divine person. It was not able to sin. But, as we have seen, its exaltation did not stop it being an unmixed and essentially unchanged human nature. It was not deified by the hypostatical union, but remained pure and separate humanity.

Such unity with the divine Son of God filled Christ's human nature with a perfection of intellectual and moral excellence beyond that of any man or woman who has ever existed. 'It pleased the Father that in him all the fulness should dwell', and 'in him dwells all the fulness of the Godhead bodily' (Colossians 1:19; 2:9). The human flesh of Jesus displayed 'the glory as of the only begotten of the Father, full of grace and truth' (John 1:14). The Father did not give 'the Spirit by measure' (John 3:34). No doubt such supernatural energy meant that his intellect and will, and every other human quality in him, were exalted and refined to a height never seen in any other creature.

To Christ the man is given a dignity and glory above every other name that is named. Not only so, but his human nature is included in the worship due to him. The grounds upon which we worship him are that he is the eternal Son of God, possessed of divine attributes. But the object of our worship is not the divine excellences in the abstract, but the divine person. That person has two natures. We bow before a man, not because any man as man is to be adored, but because this particular man is God manifest in the flesh. He is the God-Man, at whose feet we fall unashamed.

There is a further point to be mentioned while we are in this subject of Christ as the object of prayer. Because of his human nature, our Saviour is in only one place at a time. At this moment he is locally in heaven, representing us as our great High Priest. But because of his divine nature he is everywhere present, and able to hear all our prayers. He who hears us anywhere is able to understand us completely, and to sympathize fully with us, because he is a man in heaven. Should all his people pray to him at once, he sympathizes with each one. His human energies are never exhausted, because all his mediatorial functions involve both natures, and he who is a sympathetic man is also the unfailing God. The hypostatical union means that we enjoy the benefits of his humanity as often as we need, and wherever we may be, although humanity must of necessity be limited and localized.

A poor analogy

The union of Christ's two natures in his one person is a mystery which no human mind can grasp. For that very reason the reaction of some people has been to deny it. Others have responded to the mystery by attempting to give at least some explanation of it in searching for a suitable analogy.

This is why it has been popular to compare the union of the

two natures in Christ with the union of body and soul in man. On the face of it there are some points of similarity. As men and women, we are each made up of a highly organized body composed of passive matter, and a conscious, self-acting and self-determined spirit. These two are most closely united, and yet are not mixed—just as are Christ's two natures. In us body and spirit constitute one person, and the body is part of that person. The person, which is the principle of unity, does not have its seat in the body but in the spirit, so that when the spirit leaves the body, the body dies; while the person continues without the body. In the same way, in Christ the principle of unity is not in the human, but in the divine nature. In addition, the influence of the soul on the body, and the body on the soul, is a mystery, just as is the connection of the two natures in Christ and their mutual influence on each other.

Just as everything that happens in the body and in the soul is ascribed to the person, so all that takes place in the two natures of Christ is ascribed to his person. This is true although the two natures remain distinct. The attributes of the body are never ascribed to man's spirit, nor are the attributes of the spirit to the body. But the attributes of both body and spirit are common to the one person. So it is that a person is often referred to in a way which is only proper to his spiritual element, while the action he performs is decidedly something which only his body can do. The reverse is also true. This is very similar to what we have noticed concerning Christ. Often things which apply only to his human nature are ascribed to him when he is named after his divine nature, and vice-versa.

The analogy can be extended further. For instance, just as it is an honour for the body to be united with the soul, so it is an honour for the human nature of Christ to be united with the person of the eternal Son of God. And yet the analogy is defective. It does not illustrate the union of the divine and the human, of the infinite and the finite. It certainly does not illustrate the union of two spiritual natures in a single person—

Christ's divine nature, and the invisible side of his human nature. In man the union is limited to a material body and a spiritual soul. It is a wonderful union, but not as wonderful as that which took place in Christ. He had the union of body and soul which we all have — but this complete human nature was in union with an eternal divine nature, in the glorious person of the Son of God.

A view to be rejected

While we are discussing this question of the two natures of Christ we ought to mention a view which is widely held, even among those who love God's Word, but which is actually contrary to what God has revealed. It is the Lutheran view of the *communicatio idiomatum*—the communication of the properties of one of Christ's natures to the other.

This view has several forms, depending on who is presenting it. But basically it asserts that the attributes of one of Christ's natures are to be ascribed to the other, because there is an actual transference of properties from one to the other. It is felt that only by believing this can we convincingly argue for the unity of Christ's person.

Those who hold this view do not deny what we learned earlier, that the attributes of both natures can be ascribed to the one person. What is involved is an addition to that truth, out of a concern to defend the fact that Christ is but one person, and not two.

Luteran teaching

Luther and the early Lutherans taught that there was a communication of properties in both directions. Their successors insisted only on a communication from the divine nature to the human. Today Lutheran theologians generally distinguish between the operative attributes of God (such as omnipotence, omnipresence and omniscience) and his quiescent attributes (such as infinity and eternity). They teach that only the former were transferred to Christ's human nature. All schools agree that whatever communication took place occurred at the incarnation.

All of this raises the question as to how Christ can be said, for instance, to have been omnipresent during the period of his humiliation, as recorded in the Gospels. To this, Lutherans have offered a wide diversity of answers. Some say that he exercised the operative attributes, but only secretly. Others say that he did it from time to time, according to his will; or that he left them inoperative.

Inconsistencies in this teaching

Objections to this teaching have often been voiced from within the Lutheran churches themselves. For example, it has been pointed out that the whole doctrine is at variance with Luther's teaching that our Lord Jesus Christ had a genuine and truly human development. Why then did the great Reformer teach this view of the communication of properties? Was it because this view was necessary to support his own particular understanding of the Lord's Supper? He taught that Christ's human nature is omnipresent, that his body and blood are in, with and under the bread and wine. How could he have maintained this if he had not believed in the *communicatio idiomatum*? Could it be true that his view of the Supper actually led him to a wrong view of the person of Christ?

For there is no doubt that Luther's view of the communication of properties is not taught in the Bible. If we are to argue from John 3:13, 'the Son of Man who is in heaven', that omnipresence has been communicated to Christ's human nature, then we ought to argue from 1 Corinthians 2:8, 'they ... crucified the Lord of glory', that Christ's divine nature was capable of suffering. But not even Lutherans have been willing to admit that.

We cannot believe the Lutheran view *and* believe what we saw to be a self-evident truth, that Christ's two natures remain entirely distinct. How can the *attributes* of a nature be transferred, but the natures themselves remain separate? Take away the attributes and you do not *have* a nature! Besides, omnipresence is not compatible with human nature. It is simply not possible for a human, body and soul, to be present in all places at all times. How could such a thing ever be predicated of the human body of Christ? Did not the angels say of his resurrection body, 'He is not here, but is risen'? (Luke 24:6). Is not the ascended Lord he 'whom heaven must receive until the times of restoration of all things'? (Acts 3:21). Do not these verses teach clearly enough that Christ's human nature *is not* omnipresent? Such a thing could be true only if there were some mixing of the human and the divine. But these the Bible keeps strictly separate.

Modern Lutheran teaching is inconsistent. How can there be a transference of properties from the divine to the human, without there also being some transference of the human to the divine? How can some attributes be transferred, but others left behind? Do attributes have a separate existence from the nature of which they are attributes? Surely not. Does it not then follow that if some of the attributes are transferred, all of them must be? And does not that leave us where the previous paragraph left us, with two natures fused together rather than distinct, or perhaps with a Christ who in truth has only a divine nature, but not a truly human one?

In the Gospels do we *really* have a picture of a man who is everywhere present and all-knowing? And how can he be said to be in a state of humiliation if divine attributes were communicated to his *human* nature? And if that were true of him then, in what ways is he now exalted which he was not before? Does not the Lutheran view make it all but impossible to distinguish between a real state of humiliation and a state of exaltation for the God-Man?

We must reject the Lutheran view in all its forms, and return to the fold of sweet orthodoxy, which maintains from God's Word that 'There be in one and the same Jesus our Lord two natures—the divine and the human nature; and we say that these are so conjoined or united that they are not swallowed up, confounded, or mingled together, but rather united or joined together in one person (the properties of each being safe and remaining still), so that we do worship one Christ, our Lord, and not two ... Therefore we do not think nor teach that the divine nature in Christ did suffer, or that Christ, according to his human nature, is yet in the world, and so in every place.' (*The Second Helvetic Confession*, 1564, Chapter XI).

The Saviour we need

Such a Christ is exactly the Saviour we need. If he were not what we have seen him to be, we would still be lost, and perishing in our sins. How glad we should be that the 'Redeemer of God's elect is the Lord Jesus Christ, who, being the eternal Son of God, became man, and so was and continueth to be, God and man in two distinct natures, and one person, for ever' (*Westminster Shorter Catechism*, 1647).

All Christ's activity as Saviour involves both his natures, and if he were without one of these natures, or if they were ever mixed or confused, there would be no salvation for us.

It is because of his divine nature that he is a perfect Prophet. Other prophets could do no more than reflect his light, or pass on what they had received from him. All their knowledge was second hand. But the Lord Jesus Christ is God himself. His incarnation has meant that human eyes and ears have seen and heard the one who has been sent by God, who is God. We have received a perfect revelation of God, perfectly suited to our humanity. But we would have had no such Prophet, and no such revelation, if the one person had not been possessed of two distinct natures.

The human nature of Christ was necessary for him to keep God's law on our behalf, to die in our place, and to be our representative Priest and sympathetic Intercessor in heaven. At the same time, it is only the supreme dignity of his divine person which ensures that his obedience was of sufficient merit to justify sinners, and that his finite death was of infinite value, and therefore a sufficient satisfaction for divine justice. We would never have had the Priest that we need if the one person had not been possessed of two distinct natures.

In the same way the activities of his humanity and divinity are constantly and beautifully blended together in all that he does for us as King. He is the last Adam, the Second Man, the Head of a redeemed and glorified race, the First-born among many brothers, who has dominion over all his creatures. His human heart beats for us, but he acts always with divine wisdom and power, making all things work together for the accomplishment of his purposes of love.

His person, therefore, possessed of all the properties belonging to absolute deity, and an all-perfect and incomparably exalted manhood, was perfectly equipped to be our sufficient Saviour. All that he has done is to be attributed, not to one nature or the other, but to the entire person of the Theanthropos—the God-Man. In the whole of this glorious person he is ever to be obeyed and worshipped by both angels and man.

> My song shall bless the Lord of all,
> My praise shall climb to His abode;
> Thee, Saviour, by that Name I call,
> The great Supreme, the mighty God.
>
> Without beginning or decline,
> Object of faith and not of sense;
> Eternal ages saw Him shine,
> He shines eternal ages hence.
>
> As much when in the manger laid
> Almighty Ruler of the sky,

As when the six days' work He made
Filled all the morning stars with joy.

Of all the crowns Jehovah wears,
Salvation is his dearest claim;
That gracious sound, well pleased,
He hears, And owns Emmanuel for His Name.

A cheerful confidence I feel,
My well-placed hopes with joy I see;
My bosom glows with heavenly zeal,
To worship Him who died for me.

As man, he pities my complaint,
His power and truth are all divine;
He will not fail, He cannot faint;
Salvation's sure, and must be mine.

William Cowper, 1731–1800.

9

Heresies, ancient and modern

We have now studied all the main points involved in having a correct understanding of the person of the Lord Jesus Christ. He is God and man in two distinct natures, yet one person for ever. We have also seen several times why such a belief is a fundamental doctrine of the gospel. We are therefore not surprised to discover that history has witnessed repeated attempts to compromise, pervert or deny this great truth. Satan knows perfectly well that if he can discredit this doctrine, he will have destroyed the gospel.

It seems wise therefore to include in this book a brief survey of the main errors into which people have fallen, and also to look at some more recent attacks on what the Bible teaches regarding the person of Christ. This will help us to avoid falling into the same traps, and will also help to equip us to uphold this truth in the modern world. We must always remember that he who forgets the past is condemned to live it over again. A survey of misconceptions and heresies will also serve to sharpen our convictions and to make us more precise in our statement of God's truth in this day of revived errors and mushrooming cults. A careless presentation of what God has revealed is certain to lead people astray, and a chapter such as this will help to guard against this danger.

Errors concerning the person of Christ fall into three basic groups. First of all, there are those which deny the divine element in him, and hold that he was a mere man. Then there are those which deny the reality and integrity of his human nature. Finally there are those which deny the unity of the person embracing both natures. We shall look at the chief examples of these three sorts of errors. We shall then close our chapter by briefly mentioning what some modern theologians have been saying concerning our Lord Jesus Christ.

Denials of his deity

By and large, the deity of our Lord was firmly established among professing Christians for the first three centuries of the Christian church, and he was everywhere worshipped as God. So universal was this conviction that there was not felt to be any need of any definition other than those contained in Scripture. Other definitions did not appear until there was an all-out attack on his deity. We must always guard against the suggestion that the *definition* of our Lord's deity was the *creation* of faith in him as God. Where that faith was never challenged, no definition was necessary; and this is the way things remained for the best part of three hundred years.

Ebionites

In the earliest years the only group known to have denied the deity of Christ, and to have regarded him as nothing more than a mere man, was the Jewish-Gnostic Christian sect called the *Ebionites*. A party from this sect, called the Elkesaites, was particularly vocal in Syria about the middle of the second century. Some individuals also departed from orthodoxy in the early centuries, of whom the best known were two laymen from Rome, both called Theodotus: Artemon (died 180), and Paul of Samosata, who was Bishop of Antioch from AD 260 to 270, having been deposed by a council in 269. Most of these admitted that Christ had a supernatural birth, but they none the less insisted that he was simply a man who was honoured by a special divine influence. They taught that he eventually experienced a relative deification, and that this was a reward for the high quality of his earthly life and achievements.

Cerinthus

A particularly well-known heretic, at the end of the first century and at the beginning of the second, was *Cerinthus*. He held that Jesus was nothing more than a man, who was the son of Mary and Joseph. Upon him, at his baptism, came the Christ or Logos in the shape of a dove. This raised him to the dignity of the Son of God, and gave him the power to work miracles. But when he was crucified, the Logos left the man Jesus to suffer alone. He died, never to rise again.

Arius

The Ebionites and these various individuals caused little more than ripples on an otherwise untroubled surface. None of them seriously disturbed either the peace or the purity of the church. How different was the teaching of Arius, a presbyter in Alexandria, which burst on the church in the early fourth century! The wind of his teaching stirred up the smooth surface into a veritable storm. He maintained that God was but one eternal person who, before anything else was made, created in his own image his highest creature. This was his only begotten Son. Arius held that the Son was divine in only a secondary sense. He was not eternally the Son of God, and was certainly not God in the same sense as the Father. It was by the Son that everything else was made, and it was he who, much later, became a man in the person of Jesus of Nazareth.

For a considerable time it looked as if Arianism would conquer the church worldwide. Athanasius alone stood against him appealing both to the truths of the Word of God and to the beliefs of the early Christians. Mercifully, truth won the day. The Council of Nicaea of AD 325 outlawed Arianism, and insisted that the Lord Jesus Christ was 'very God of very God, begotten, not made, being of one substance with the Father'. Had Arianism triumphed, biblical Christianity would have been destroyed.

For centuries after the Arian controversy there was no group in the church which openly denied the deity of the Lord Jesus Christ. And yet Arianism has never died a final death, and has re-emerged in history from time to time. Those who call themselves *Jehovah's Witnesses* are a modern form of Arian, believing exactly what Arius did concerning the person of Christ. Most other modern cults also expressly deny the deity of the Saviour. We must ever be on our guard against their teachings, and must remember how error gets a foothold in the life of the churches. Arius would never have had so much influence if Origen (185–255) had not unwittingly prepared the way for him by teaching that although the Son is a glorious and divine person, he is not God in quite the same sense as the Father. He thus sowed the thought that there are ranks within the Godhead, and this made it easier for Arius to go a step further. Origen's view, later known as Semi-Arianism, could not have got off the ground if Tertullian (approximately 160–240) had not already expressed a doubt about the equality of the Son of God with the Father. His comparatively small error paved the way for the dangerous heresies of later years, and shows to us the immense importance of being precise in our doctrinal statements.

Nor are the Ebionites completely dead. Their view that Christ was nothing more than a mere man was held by the *Socinians* who were prominent in Europe during the sixteenth century, and is held by the *Unitarians*, who continue to this day. During the nineteenth century, when the Bible was being attacked and the miracles denied, the same belief found its way into almost all of the major denominations. There are still large numbers of 'liberal' or 'modernist' ministers who believe in this way, and some of them have been increasingly vocal in recent years. This is especially true of those who are publicly identified with the ecumenical movement and its expression in those bodies connected with the World Council of Churches.

Denials of his humanity

Virtually all parties in the early church which denied the real humanity of our Lord Jesus Christ were of Gnostic origin. *The Gnostics* had existed from the earliest times, and were spread throughout the known world by the early second century. They held that God was one essence and one person, and that from him emanated lesser divine beings, by which he maintained contact with the world. These are called 'aeons', and Christ was one of the greatest. Such intermediaries are necessary because matter, which is self-existent, is intrinsically evil, and God can therefore have no direct contact with it.

The Docetae

Gnostic teaching became highly developed among *the Docetae* who plagued the church in the fourth century. Believing all matter to be evil, they proclaimed that Christ's human nature, body and soul, was a mere phantom. He appeared to be a man, but was not. His humanity had no substantial existence. It was nothing more than a vision, an illusion through which the Logos chose to manifest himself for a time to mankind. He was not born and did not die. Such a belief became very widespread, and for a time constituted almost as big a threat to Christianity as did Arianism, albeit from an altogether different angle. It was eventually overcome, and yet was still being taught as late as the Middle Ages by individuals such as Peter the Lombard (1100–1164).

Apollinaris

Another attack on the integrity of Christ's human nature also came in the fourth century, from *Apollinaris*, who was Bishop of Laodicaea around 370. Although apparently orthodox in all other points, and reputed for his learning, Apollinaris' view of man was derived more from Plato than from the Scriptures. He taught that man consisted of a body (*soma*), an animal soul (*psyche*) and a human spirit (*pneuma*), all comprehended in one person. In Christ, he said, although he had a true human body and an animal soul, the divine Logos or Word took the place of the human *pneuma*. Apollinaris fully accepted Christ's deity, but asserted that in him the rational human spirit was replaced by his divine being. This human spirit, he argued, was the seat of sin, and therefore the sinless Son of Man could not have had one.

In this way Apollinaris denied that Christ had a *complete* human nature. But if Jesus did not take our nature upon him, how could he have redeemed us? Apollinaris' speculation certainly got rid of the difficulties attending a co-existence of two rational, self-determining spirits in one person. But it destroyed the revealed truth that we have studied, that Christ is at once very man and very God. It also denied that we have a Saviour who 'was in all points tempted as we are …' (Hebrews 4:15). Apollinarianism was rightly condemned by the Council of Constantinople in AD 381.

Christian Science

Unfortunately, condemnation by a council does not mean that a heresy has gone out of existence. It is true that there have been very few people or groups since Constantinople who have denied Christ's real humanity. The heresy is almost unknown, but not quite. *Christian Science* still holds to it. 'Christ is incorporeal, spiritual,' wrote Mary Baker Eddy in her *Miscellaneous Writings*. Her movement denies the reality of Christ's body and the integrity of his humanity. We must remind ourselves that it is precisely such a view that the apostle John so emphatically refuted when he wrote, 'And every spirit that does not confess that Jesus Christ has come in the flesh is not of God. And this is the spirit of the antichrist, which you have heard was coming, and is now already in the world' (1 John 4:3).

Denials of the one person or the two natures

From time to time church history has witnessed those who have been so keen to stress that our Lord's two natures were distinct and unmodified, that they have thrown into the shade the equally revealed fact of the unity of his person. It is hard to call such a loss of balance a heresy, because it does not specifically deny any scriptural doctrine. But it is most certainly an error and exceedingly dangerous.

Nestorius

This tendency became conspicuous in the theology which emanated from Antioch in the fourth and fifth centuries, as a result of the writings of Theodore of Mopsuestia. When *Nestorius*, who had been a monk at Antioch, became Patriarch of Constantinople, matters came to a head. In seeking to defend the complete humanity of our Lord he expressed his disapproval of the phrase 'Mother of God' as applied to the virgin Mary, insisting that she had given birth to Christ, but not to God. He was able to make this distinction because he believed that the divine and the human natures of Christ ought to be distinctly separated. Our Lord's personality was twofold and the two natures were distinct in such a way that he was virtually regarded by Nestorius as two persons, the one divine and the other human, rather than as one person in two natures. His deity indwelt his humanity, but the two were in no way joined. Cyril of Alexandria, who opposed Nestorius, held to the orthodox doctrine that two distinct natures were in perfect union in Christ, and in AD 431 the Council of Ephesus condemned Nestorius, and thus also condemned the whole Antiochene school, of which he was a representative.

Eutyches

A little later the city of Constantinople heard a view which went to the completely opposite extreme. *Eutyches*, the abbot, finding that Nestorianism had not completely disappeared, energetically led continuing opposition against it. In doing so, he fell into the error of confounding the two natures of Christ. He came to hold that Christ had but a single nature, either from a fusing of the two, or from the absorption of the human into the divine. Mistakenly supposing that he had Cyril as an ally, he specifically denied that there were two natures in Christ. He and his followers became known as *Monophysites* and were condemned by the Council of Chalcedon of AD 451, to which we have so often alluded.

Although alienated from the orthodox church, the Monophysites continued for some time afterwards. The Emperor Heraclius made an attempt to reunite them with mainstream Christianity by suggesting a compromise. They should adopt the statements of Chalcedon, with the amendment that in consequence of the hypostatical union there was but one divine-human energy, and one will, in Christ. Those who held to this view are known to us as *Monothelites*. In opposition to them the sixth ecumenical Council of Constantinople of AD 681, with the co-operation of the Bishop of Rome, adopted as the orthodox doctrine that in Christ there were *two* wills and two energies, but declared that the human will must always be viewed as subordinate to the divine. With this decision, the definition of what the whole Christian church believes concerning the person of the Lord Jesus Christ was closed.

Adoptionism

But even this did not prevent yet one more serious heresy arising. This was the view of Felix, *Bishop of Urgella*, now known as *adoptionism*. Like all heresies, it arose because the simple statements of Scripture were not accepted, and a solution to the problems Scripture raises was sought in human reason. Felix sought to preserve the unity of Christ's person by suggesting that although he was the Son of God as to his divine nature, he was only the adopted Son of God as far as his human nature was concerned. This adoptive sonship did not begin with the natural birth of Christ, but began at his baptism and was consummated at his resurrection. It was a spiritual birth that made the man Jesus the adopted Son of God. The church was quick to see that this view was not true to the New Testament. The new teaching did not preserve the unity of Christ's person, as it claimed, but rather endangered it. It was decisively condemned by the Synod of Frankfurt in AD 794.

The nineteenth century

The Middle Ages did not bring any further definition of the doctrine of the person of Christ. Occasionally individuals or small groups departed from orthodoxy, but the existing definitions were sufficient to expose them for the errors that they were. All these errors were either revivals or modifications of heresies we have discussed.

Nor did things change at the Reformation. Although poles apart on countless points, both the church of Rome and the churches of the Reformation subscribed to the doctrine of Christ as formulated at Chalcedon. The only new feature to arise during this period was the emergence of the Lutheran view of the *communicatio idiomatum* which we have already discussed.

The historical Jesus

It was at the beginning of the nineteenth century that a great change took place in the study of the person of Christ. The previous century had seen an increasing interest in the study of the historical Jesus. Now a distinction was drawn between '*the historical Jesus*' who had actually existed, as set forth by the Gospels, and the Christ of *theology*, set forth in the creeds and confessions of the church. Scholars thought less and less of a supernatural Christ, and spoke of a human Jesus. They abandoned the doctrine of the two natures and wrote of a divine man. *Schleiermacher* and *Hegel* were prominent names in this new development. For both of them, Christ never rose above being a human teacher, though he was unique, either because of his perfect sense of union with the divine, or as the expression of the oneness which exists between God and man. The first six chapters of this book have shown us a Christ radically different from these human speculations. The Christ of the biblical record and the theological Christ of the creeds is the *same* Christ. The church's statements only draw together all the various strands of biblical data in order to formulate a *definition* of what God's Word, in its totality, reveals.

Kenosis

It was also during the nineteenth century that there arose the theory of *kenosis*. This was an entirely new attempt to reconstruct the doctrine of the person of Christ. The term is derived from Philippians 2:7, which teaches that Christ 'emptied (*ekenosen*) himself, taking the form of a bond-servant' (NASB). The Kenoticists took this to mean that the Word or Logos was literally changed into a man. He laid aside his omnipotence, omniscience and omnipresence, and even his divine self-consciousness. He then, throughout his human life, increased in wisdom and power, until at last he again became God. This kenotic theory appeared in a wide diversity of forms, and enjoyed considerable popularity, first in Germany and then in England. It is still alive in some circles today. Its aim was to maintain the reality of Christ's manhood and to emphasize how great was his humiliation in becoming poor for our sakes.

However, this theory is open to serious objections and cannot be held by those who bow to the authority of Scripture. The verb appealed to in Philippians 2:7 is used four other times in the New Testament (Romans 4:14; 1 Corinthians 1:17; 9:15; 2 Corinthians 9:3), but never in the sense of 'emptied'. Linguistic integrity drives us to translate the verse exactly as it appears in the New King James Version: 'But made himself of no reputation, taking the form of a servant …' The Authorized Version's rendering of this verse is almost exactly the same. The verse is teaching that Christ did not assert his divine prerogative, but made himself of no account, and took the form of a servant. It was not his 'being in the form of God' (v. 6) that he laid aside, but his being at a level of equality with God. The verse specifically says so. He did not cease to be what he always was, but exchanged one *state* for another. Instead of exercising his right to command, he put himself in a state of subjection where he was called upon to render obedience. No doubt this economic subordination caused our Lord to sustain new relations to the Father and the Holy Spirit, but it in no way altered his essential deity.

Kenotic theory is based on a pantheistic conception of God, where God and man are not regarded as absolutely different, but where it is believed that one can change into the other. The biblical line of demarcation between the two is obliterated. It is also a plain contradiction of the clearly revealed fact that God cannot change (Malachi 3:6; James 1:17). Not only so, but it destroys the doctrine of the Trinity. The humanized Son, self-emptied of his divine attributes, could no longer be a divine subsistence in the trinitarian life. It falls into the same error as that of the Lutherans, examined earlier, in thinking that divine attributes can be stripped away, but that the divine *being* can somehow be left intact and unaffected. It overlooks the Bible's teaching that our Lord *did* have divine attributes during the period recorded by the Gospels. Have we not seen that he was then real and absolute God? Added to this, the theory does not even accomplish what it sets out to do. How is the real manhood of Christ assured by believing that a reduced Logos took the place of the human soul? The Christ of kenotic theory is neither God nor man, but, as B. B. Warfield put it, 'just shrunken deity'. He is a million miles removed from the glorious God-Man set before us in Holy Scripture.

Gradual incarnation

Another nineteenth-century theory contradictory to God's Word is that of *gradual incarnation*, which aimed to escape the errors of the Kenoticists, but to do full justice to the humanity of Christ.

According to this theory, the incarnation was not an act which took place at the conception of Jesus. It was a gradual process by which the Logos joined himself in ever-increasing measure to the unique and representative man, Jesus Christ.

The union was finally consummated at the time of the resurrection and the result was a God-Man with a single will and a single personality. The seat of this personality was the human Jesus, but the Logos gave that personality a divine quality. None of this finds any support in the New Testament. The idea of two persons increasingly becoming one is nothing more than a revived and sophisticated form of Nestorianism. The view that a human Jesus is the real personality, and constitutes his real ego, was found in several other nineteenth-century views of Christ. Their proponents saw him as a human who became divine in some sense, or who, at least, had a subconscious awareness of divinity. The New Testament's view could not be more different. The ego of the Logos was pre-existent. He was the eternal Son of God who became man.

Albrecht Ritschl

But the nineteenth-century name which exercised the greatest influence on modern thinking regarding the person of Christ is undoubtedly that of *Albrecht Ritschl* (1822–1889). Christ, he said, was a mere man; but in the light of what he did we rightly call him God, because that is the value he has for us. We can rule out his pre-existence, his incarnation and his virgin birth. These are irrelevancies to personal faith. But his teaching, example and unique influence move us to enter the Christian community, and to live lives motivated entirely by love. These views are little different from those of Paul of Samosata. But by Ritschl's influence they have percolated into almost every corner of Christendom.

These, then, were the sort of ideas influencing people's minds as the twentieth century began. None of them could have gained any acceptance if professing Christians had remained submissive to the Scriptures and had continued to maintain that what we believe about the person of Christ is to be decided by revelation, and not by human reasoning. As it was, the nineteenth century was the era for attacking the Bible, and for exalting human philosophy. Hand in hand with a forsaking of the Scriptures went a departure from the historic creeds and confessions. The two stand or fall together, because the latter are the expression of the former. But those who felt that they could disbelieve the Bible and renounce the church's statements of its faith, and yet keep their Christ, were sadly mistaken. They have not caused love for Christ to increase, but to grow cold. The fruit of their activity has been that countless men and women have turned their backs on him. Apostasy in the churches has ushered in an age of unprecedented unbelief. The cynical world has little but contempt for those who appear to be kissing their Saviour, but are in fact seeking to advance themselves by handing him over to his enemies.

Theology today

Once the soil of fallen human reason has been fertilized with unashamed disbelief of God's Word, there is no telling what theories will grow there. In today's world the truth about the person of Christ is still nursed in many minds and loved in many hearts, but only because of the grace of God. It is a tender plant surrounded by a veritable jungle of human theories and interpretations, which look as if they will choke it out of existence. May God use this book to help revive the languishing plant! And may it inspire the strong and the competent to put an axe to the encroaching undergrowth!

Karl Barth

Contemporary theology, as distinct from that of the nineteenth century, was born in 1919, with the publication of a commentary on Romans by *Karl Barth* (1886–1968). Barth has without doubt been the most influential theologian of modern times, and his views have affected the professing church on every continent. As a result, contemporary theology has become world theology. Modern views are not hidden away in a corner. Wherever we may be, we are certain to meet them.

There is much in Barth's theology which is important and right, but his view of the person of Christ should alarm us. To him it was a matter of no importance whether the historical facts concerning Jesus in the Gospels are reliable or not. Faith is not based on historical facts, but on a personal encounter with Christ. The recorded fact of his resurrection, for example, is worthless to the Christian. What matters is that we should have an encounter with him. By such statements Barth cuts Christianity from history, and so destroys its very basis. To him the genuine historicity of the redemptive work of Christ as the foundation of the Christian gospel is open to question.

Barth none the less admitted that Jesus Christ is very God, although he was not willing to admit the humiliation of the man Jesus. He refused to accept that in Christ there was an estate of humiliation followed chronologically by an estate of exaltation. 'What sense can there be in talking of a man as humiliated?' he enquired. 'That is natural to man. And what sense can there be in talking of God as exalted? That is natural to God.' This is not the time and place to pursue Barth's teaching further. We have said enough to show that for him historical definitions concerning the person of Christ counted for nothing. Modern theology began with a repudiation of Chalcedon.

Brunner and Bultmann

Apart from serious differences concerning general revelation and the reality of the virgin birth, similar to Barth's theology was that of *Emil Brunner* (1889–1966). More radical than Barth, but equally influential, was *Rudolf Bultmann* (1884–1976). Like Barth and Brunner, Bultmann did not see the Bible as the inspired Word of God in any objective sense. His main contention was that the Gospels do not give us a true and authentic view of

Jesus. They express, rather, what the early church saw him to be. We must dismantle the framework of the story, as composed by those first Christians, and get behind it to see what the real Christ was like.

Bultmann believed that the real truth about Jesus lies largely in those passages recording his teaching, not in the record of his deeds. He did not doubt that Jesus had once lived, but doubted whether we can know much more about him than that. The authentic snatches of his teaching which the early church possessed were made artificially into a coherent narrative by means of invented historical details of sequence, time, place etc. These must be discounted, and all our attention must be given to the little information that remains when we have stripped this away. Bultmann thus ignored the fact that the New Testament was entirely written by Christ's apostles, or under their supervision. He allowed us no significant data by which we may formulate a doctrine of the person of Christ. He saw the pre-existent and glorious person of the New Testament as a myth invented by the first believers, for the sake of their preaching, but which has no validity for men and women today. We must dig behind the thought-forms and embellishments of the early church, and present the Christ we find there in a way which is meaningful to twenty-first-century people.

Bultmann, like Barth, destroyed the foundation of Christianity in history. He ignored the fact that the gospel message of the early church centred on the person and work of a historical Christ, and reduced his influence to nothing. He rejected the supernaturalism of historic Christianity and proclaimed a system which, despite some overlapping of terms, was a religion of his own making.

This is a point which needs considerable emphasis. Modern theology is not a perversion of historic Christianity. We cannot even call it a departure from it, for it is hard to see that the two have a common starting-point. It is something entirely different, foreign, alien and other. It uses many of the terms used by the Christian faith of history, but injects into them a totally different meaning. It claims to speak of the Lord Jesus Christ, but its Christ has little in common with the Christ of the Scriptures *other than the spelling of his name*. The terms of reference of the historic creeds and confessions have little meaning to modern theologies. They are irrelevancies. They are like statements from another world. The reverse is also true. Those schooled in a biblical view of Christ and embracing Chalcedon's definitions find modern theology almost impossible to comprehend. It makes no sense. It strikes no note in the heart. It speaks another, and unknown, language.

Paul Tillich

A striking example of this is the theology of *Paul Tillich* (1886–1965). To him religion was not a matter of certain beliefs and practices, but was the point at which a person is 'ultimately concerned'. He therefore rejected all traditional formulae concerning the person and work of Christ. He regarded the statement, 'God has become man' not only as paradoxical, but as nonsensical. To him the Gospel narratives were mostly legendary, and the resurrection of Christ of no importance. What mattered was not whether Christ rose from the dead or not, but whether his dignity was restored in the minds of his disciples. To Tillich Christ was nothing of himself, but was important as the symbol in whom estrangement from the ground of our being is overcome.

Oscar Cullmann

Humble believers understand what the Bible is saying about Christ and can identify with the old creeds and confessions. But they cannot usually make head nor tail of such views as that. Much more comprehensible to them are the writings of *Oscar Cullmann* (b. 1902), but this is because he so very frequently appeals to Scripture in his studies. However, although his research has given us some valuable insights into the Christology of the New Testament, he is still unwilling to assure us that we have there a totally reliable account of the life and teaching of Jesus. He also insists that the New Testament has no real interest in who Christ is, in and of himself, in his person. By implication, therefore, he denies his deity. Cullmann is certainly quite unconcerned to present Christ as one who shares in the trinitarian life of the Godhead. In the final analysis it becomes evident that his Christ is not the Christ of the Scriptures whom we love and adore.

Dietrich Bonhoeffer

What other 'Christs' have been presented to us in our time? *Dietrich Bonhoeffer* (1906–1945) applauded 'the man for others', while *John Robinson* (1919–1984) in his 1963 best seller *Honest to God* told us of one who is 'a window into God at work'. *Alfred North Whitehead* (1861–1947) and the advocates of 'process theology' told us of one who is the only man in whom God has worked, but openly denied the idea that he was God incarnate. *Pierre Teilhard de Chardin* (1881–1955) invented a Christ who is the inner principle and consummation of the evolutionary process. *Jurgen Moltmann* (b. 1926) has a Christ who is someone to mention from time to time, whose physical resurrection is disbelieved, and upon whom his 'theology of hope' in no way depends. *Wolfart Pannenberg* (b. 1928) contradicts him, and tells the world that Christ certainly rose from the dead. For a moment our hearts are lifted, and we wonder if a new champion of the apostolic faith has emerged. But we are at once plunged into disappointment when Pannenberg speaks of a fallible Christ— one who was mistaken in thinking that his resurrection would coincide with the end of the world and the resurrection of all believers.

In the hall of modern theology a thousand voices shout a thousand theories in a never-dying Babel of confusion. The world outside, hearing no clear and authoritative voice, covers its ears from the noise, and goes about its business. From the little it has been able to pick up it has concluded that no one is sure whether Christ existed or not, but, whichever way it is, Christianity is something to do with following his example. The church's own activities lead it to believe that this example is best followed when we engage in political activity or do social work among the poor. And so a world perishes unreminded of its offences against its holy Creator and Judge, and ignorant that in the God-Man there is an all-sufficient Saviour for the repentant.

It is time for those who know the truth to raise their voices so loudly that modern theology's voices, in comparison, seem like silence. God's Word is clear about the person of the Lord Jesus Christ. The old creeds and confessions have summarized the truth admirably. With unwavering tones we can tell the world that 'The Son of God, the second person in the Trinity, being very and eternal God, of one substance with the Father, did, when the fulness of time was come, take upon him man's nature, and all the essential properties and common infirmities thereof, yet without sin: being conceived by the power of the Holy Ghost in the womb of the virgin Mary, of her substance. So that two whole, perfect, and distinct natures, the Godhead and the manhood, were inseparably joined together in one person, without conversion, composition, or confusion. Which person is very God and very man, yet one Christ, the only mediator between God and man' (*Westminster Confession*, VIII, 2).

> God the Father's only Son,
> And with Him in glory one,
> One in wisdom, one in might,
> Absolute and infinite;
> Jesu, I believe in Thee,
> Thou art Lord and God to me.
>
> Preacher of eternal peace,
> Christ, anointed to release,
> Calling man from error's night
> Into truth's eternal light;

Jesu, I believe in Thee,
Christ the Prophet sent to me.

Low in deep Gethsemane,
High on dreadful Calvary,
In the garden, on the cross,
Making good our utter loss;
Jesu, I believe in Thee,
Priest and Sacrifice for me.

Ruler of Thy ransomed race,
And protector by Thy grace,
Leader through our earthly strife,
And the goal of all our life;
Jesu, I believe in Thee,
Christ, the King of kings to me.

Samuel John Stone
1839–1900.

Postscript

In these chapters we have examined the wonderful person of our Lord Jesus Christ, and it has been emphasized that he is the eternal God—as the hymn-writer Charles Wesley so well expressed:

Let earth and heaven combine,
Angels and men agree,
To praise in songs divine
The incarnate Deity;

Our God contracted to a span,
Incomprehensibly made man.

Our Saviour did not shrink back from assuming perfect manhood into his being. Anselm's question, *Cur Deus Homo?*—Why did God become man?—is answered in that he became man so as to make full atonement for the sins of all those who would turn to him in repentance and faith. For our salvation, Christ had to be fully man and fully God.

As we have seen in this book, many views of Christ are deficient at one point or another, and we must strive always to be biblical in our thinking and in the way we express this truth. In recent years, some extremist movements have mistakenly tried to exalt Christ above the Father. Others have so emphasized his ability to perform miracles that they have portrayed him only in the role as some kind of wonder-working superman.

There have been notable deficiencies in the teaching of many influential proponents of the Word of Faith movement with respect to the person and work of Christ, such as one view that Christ was conquered by Satan at the cross, and another view that he came as a man to be the model of health and wealth for modern believers. Authors such as McConnell and Hanegraaff[1] have documented clearly and carefully some of these erroneous and blasphemous views of our Lord's person and work.

The magnificence of God's grace is expressed at its pinnacle in the Lord Jesus Christ. To him be glory in the church, now, and for evermore.

The Publishers

Endnote

1 See D. McConnell, *A different Gospel* (Hendrickson Publishers, 1995); and H.Hanegraaff, *Christianity in Crisis* (Harvest House Publishers, 1997).

Appendix 1
The Creed of Chalcedon

The oldest and most widely accepted statement of all the main points involved in the doctrine of the person of Christ is that drawn up at Chalcedon, on the Bosphorus, opposite Constantinople, in October AD 451. The Emperor Marcianus called the fourth General Council to put down the Nestorian and Eutychian heresies. The council consisted of 630 bishops, and the main part of the 'Definition of Faith' on which they agreed follows. It is a careful statement in systematic form of the pure teaching of the Scriptures, and has stood ever since as the norm of thought and teaching regarding the person of Christ. It is the commonly received faith of the whole Christian church, and has been incorporated into countless creeds and confessions, as well as providing the basis for a large number of devotional writings and hymns.

'We, then, following the holy fathers, all with one consent, teach men to confess, one and the same Son, our Lord Jesus Christ; the same perfect in Godhead and also perfect in Manhood; truly God, and truly Man, of a reasonable soul and body; consubstantial with the Father according to the Godhead, and consubstantial with us according to the Manhood; in all things like unto us without sin; begotten before all ages of the Father according to the Godhead, and in these latter days, for us and for our salvation, born of Mary the virgin Mother of God according to the Manhood. He is one and the same Christ, Son, Lord, Only-begotten, existing in two natures without mixture, without change, without division, without separation; the diversity of the two natures not being at all destroyed by their union, but the peculiar properties of each nature being preserved, and concurring to one person and one subsistence, not parted or divided into two persons, but one and the same Son, and Only-begotten, God the Word, the Lord Jesus Christ; as the prophets from the beginning have declared concerning Him, and as the Lord Jesus Christ Himself hath taught us, and as the Creed of the holy fathers has delivered to us.'

Appendix 2
The Athanasian Creed

This creed is so named because the opening words *Quicunque vult* ('Whosoever wishes' are traditionally ascribed to Athanasius, Bishop of Alexandria from about AD 328 to 373, and the great champion of biblical orthodoxy against Arianism. The creed itself is of a later date, being drawn up after the controversies concerning the person of Christ were closed, and after the definitions of Ephesus and Chalcedon had become established. It was probably produced in North Africa between the fifth and eighth centuries by those influenced by Augustine of Hippo.

The *Athanasian Creed* is a magnificent statement of the faith of the church regarding the great mysteries of the Trinity, and the person of Christ. It is accepted by the whole Christian church, though many Christians have reservations about its 'damnatory clauses'. It is felt that such statements should never be attached to what is a purely human document, and especially to one which makes such fine distinctions on such deep subjects.

'1. Whosoever wishes to be saved, it is above all necessary for him to hold the Catholic faith. 2. Which, unless each one shall preserve perfect and inviolate, he shall certainly perish for ever. 3. But the Catholic faith is this, that we worship one God in trinity, and trinity in unity. 4. Neither confounding the persons, nor separating the substance. 5. For the person of the Father is one, of the Son another, and of the Holy Ghost another. 6. But of the Father, of the Son, and of the Holy Ghost there is one divinity, equal glory and co-eternal majesty. 7. What the Father is, the same is the Son, and the Holy Ghost. 8. The Father is uncreated, the Son uncreated, the Holy Ghost uncreated. 9. The Father is immense, the Son immense, the Holy Ghost immense. 10. The Father is eternal, the Son eternal, the Holy Ghost eternal. 11. And yet there are not three eternals, but one eternal. 12. So there are not three [beings] uncreated, nor three immense, but one uncreated and one immense. 13. In like manner the Father is omnipotent, the Son is omnipotent, the Holy Ghost is omnipotent. 14. And yet there are not three omnipotents, but one omnipotent. 15. Thus the Father is God, the Son is God, the Holy Ghost is God. 16. And yet there are not three Gods, but one God. 17. Thus the Father is Lord, the Son is Lord, and the Holy Ghost is Lord. 18. And yet there are not three Lords, but one Lord. 19. Because as we are thus compelled by Christian verity to confess each person severally to be God and Lord; so we are prohibited by the Catholic religion from saying that there are three Gods or Lords. 20. The Father was made from none, nor created, nor begotten. 21. The Son is from the Father alone, neither made, nor created, but begotten. 22. The Holy Ghost is from the Father and the Son, neither made, nor created, nor begotten, but proceeding. 23. Therefore there is one Father, not three fathers, one Son, not three sons, one Holy Ghost, not three Holy Ghosts. 24. And in this trinity no one is first or last, no one is greater or less. 25. But all the three co-eternal persons are co-equal among themselves; so that through all, as is above said, both unity in trinity, and trinity in unity is to be worshipped. 26. Therefore, he who wishes to be saved must think thus concerning the trinity. 27. But it is necessary to eternal salvation that he should also faithfully believe the incarnation of our Lord Jesus Christ. 28. It is, therefore, true faith that we believe and confess that our Lord Jesus Christ is both God and Man. 29. He is God, generated from eternity from the substance of the Father; man, born in time from the substance of his mother. 30. Perfect God, perfect man, subsisting of a rational soul and human flesh. 31. Equal to the Father in respect to his divinity, less than the Father in respect to his humanity. 32. Who, although he is God and man, is not two but one Christ. 33. But one, not from the conversion of his divinity into flesh, but from the assumption of his humanity into God. 34. One not at all from confusion of substance, but from unity of person. 35. For as a rational soul and flesh is one man, so God and man is one Christ. 36. Who suffered for our salvation, descended into hell, the third day rose from the dead. 37. Ascended to heaven, sitteth at the right hand of God the Father omnipotent, whence he shall come to judge the living and the dead. 38. At whose coming all men shall rise again with their bodies, and shall render an account for their own works. 39. And they who have done well shall go into life eternal; they who have done evil into eternal fire. 40. This is the Catholic faith, which, unless a man shall faithfully and firmly believe, he cannot be saved.'

Scripture Index

Genesis

1:1	30
1:26	141
3:15	94
3:22	141
11:7	141
16:7–13	86
17:7	94
18	86
22:11–15	86
28:13	87
31:11,13	87
32:24	88
32:30	88
48:15–16	87
49:10	94

Exodus

3	87
13:21	87
14:19	87
24:9–10	90
28:9,12,21,29	126

Numbers

21:5–6	28

Deuteronomy

4:33,36,39	88

Judges

6:11,12,14,16	87
6:19–22	87
13:3,9,22	87
13:6,10	87
13:15–23	87

1 Kings

2:19	125
8:27	71

Nehemiah

9:13	88

Psalms

2	34, 92
2:6,7,10–12	92
8:4	102
16:9–11	94
22	94
22:1	94
22:6,9–12	94
22:7–8	94
22:14	94
22:16	94
22:17	94
22:18	94
40:6–10	94
45	35
45:6–7	28, 68
50:12	104
68:18	61, 67
69:21	94, 104
102:24–27	29
103:19	30
110	92
110:1	125
118:17–23	94
121:4	104
135:6	72
139:2–5	72

139:7–10	71
145:9	30
146:3	102

Ecclesiastes

12:14	75

Isaiah

6:1–10	29
6:1–12	89
6:3	31
7:14	42, 91, 94, 98
7:15	42
7:16	42
8:8	42
8:13–14	29
9:1	43
9:1–6	29
9:1–7	91
9:6	35, 94
9:6–7	43
40:3	51
40:28	71, 104
44:6	29, 71
45:23	72
50:6	94
52:7	70
53	94
53:9	94
63:7–9	88

Jeremiah

23:5–6	94
23:6	36

Daniel

2:20	73
4:35	72
7:13	102
9:24–27	94

Hosea

12:4–5	88

Joel

2:32	70

Micah

5:2	33, 91, 94

Habakkuk

1:12	71

Haggai

2:9	94

Zechariah

2:10–11	90
9:9	94
11:12–13	94
12:10	94
13:7	36, 90

Malachi

3:1	29, 36, 93, 94
3:2	36
3:6	30, 72, 174
4:5–6	36

Matthew

1:1–17	99
1:18	43
1:20	98
1:20–23	44
1:22–23	41
1:23	39, 98, 152
2:1–8	91
2:1–23	99
2:6	33
4:1–11	109
4:2	104
4:14–16	29, 35, 91
5:18,20,22	45
7:21–23	75
7:22	28
7:28–29	45
8:24	104
8:29	53
9:4	55
9:10–13	105
9:27–33	56
9:36	109
11:7–15	36
11:10	29
11:19	101, 105
11:27	34, 49
11:29	116
12:8	102
12:31–32	49
14:33	57
16:16	49
16:21	55
17:5	52
18:20	56, 71

Scripture Index

21:18	104	10:14	109	10:22	73
22:29	91	10:21	109	11:4	114
22:43–44	35, 92	11:12	104	17:11–19	56
24:27	128	13:32	108	19:10	102
24:37	128	14:8	104	19:41–44	109
25:31–32	130	14:34	107	22:31–34	55
25:31–46	75	16:19	61	22:44	105, 107
26:26	104			23:46	57, 107
26:31	36			24:6	158

Luke

26:38	107	1:15–17	51	24:18–19	104
26:39	107	1:30–35	43	24:25	122
26:47–50	104	1:35	98	24:31,36	121
26:63	50	1:76–77	51	24:37–43	120
26:63–66	59	2:7	99	24:39	106
26:64	124	2:8–20	99	24:42	106
26:65	50	2:10–11	50	24:50	123
27:62–66	59	2:11	28	24:50–51	61
28:1–2	121	2:21–35	99		
28:18	73	2:40	100, 108		

John

28:19	77	2:41–52	100	1:1	24, 33
28:20	56, 71	2:48–49	44	1:1–2	33
		2:52	108	1:1–2,14	142
		3:22	52	1:1–3	25

Mark

		3:23–38	99	1:3,10	30
1:1–9	93	5:8	28, 57	1:14	32, 39, 40, 52, 110, 153
1:2	36	5:16	109	1:14–18	33
1:24	53, 114	5:25–26	56	1:15,30	24
1:27	53	6:8	55	1:18	32, 40, 88
1:35	109	6:12	109	1:22–23	51
2:7–10	56	7:14–15	56	1:23	36
3:5	109	7:16	56	1:29–30	52
3:21	100	7:44–46	104	1:29–34	37
4:41	56	9:18,28	109	1:29,34	52
5:41–42	56	9:43	56	1:47	55
6:3	100	9:47	55	2:19–21	119
7:34–35	56	10:21	108, 109	2:24–25	55
9:33–37	55				

3:13	23, 56, 101, 144, 157	8:58	25, 47, 146	19:38–42	105
3:16	32, 34	10	46	20:5–8	121
3:18	32	10:17	81	20:13	106, 121
3:31	24	10:17–18	58	20:15	104
3:34	98, 153	10:22–42	48	20:17	106
3:35	73	10:28	74	20:19,26	121
4:6	104	10:30	89	20:24–29	55
4:7	104	11:5	109	20:25	60
4:9	103	11:25–26	74	20:26–28	60
4:17–19	55	11:33–36	108	20:27	106, 121
4:25–26	49	11:43–44	56	20:28	28
5:8–9	56	12:27	107, 115	20:29	60
5:16–47	45	12:37–41	31	21:4–5	104
5:17,21,36	56	12:39–41	29, 89	21:4,12	121
5:21,25–27	74	12:41	31	21:9–14	106
5:22	130	12:45	89		
5:22,28–29	75	13:10–11	55		

Acts

5:23	57, 77	13:13–17	116	1:3	122
5:27	130	13:21	107	1:9	61
5:28–29	74, 129	13:23	104	1:9–10	123
5:36	89	14:3	128	1:11	123, 128
5:39–40	91	14:9	27, 89	2:22	110
6:46	89	14:10–11	48	2:22,33	124
6:62	24, 61, 101, 144	14:23	71	2:27	73
6:68–69	49	14:28	101	2:32–33	74
6:70–71	55	14:30	114	2:33–36	124
7:10–14	103	15:14–15	107	2:34–36	69
7:27	99	15:24	101	3:18	115
7:32,45–46	45	16:7	74	3:20–21	127
7:33	61	16:28	23	3:21	158
7:37–39	61	17:5	24	5:31	124
7:42	33, 91	18:1–11	58	7:31	87
8	46	19:5	105	7:38	88
8:11	56	19:28	104	7:56	124, 131
8:39–40	101	19:30	57, 105	7:59–60	77
8:46	113	19:32–35	105	9:4–6	124

Scripture Index

9:20	70	15:35–44	119	2:5–7	26
9:20,22	54	15:45	114	2:5–11	26
10:42	75, 130	15:47	24	2:6	33
13:23	99	15:51–52	129	2:7	41, 173
13:33	35			2:8	105
13:38	110	**2 Corinthians**		2:9	77, 124
16:31	60	3:18	114	2:9–10	130
17:31	75, 110, 130	4:4	33	2:10–11	73, 130
20:28	58, 143	4:6	89	2:11	78
		5:10	75	3:8	77
Romans		5:19	58	3:20–21	74
1:3	34	5:21	113	3:21	72, 114, 129
1:3–4	141	8:9	24		
1:3–5	54	9:3	173	**Colossians**	
1:4	59	9:6	174	1:13–14	143
4:14	173	12:8	77	1:14–20	34
8:3	34, 54, 103, 111, 142	13:14	77	1:15	32, 33
9:5	29, 68, 142, 146			1:16–17	30
9:33	29	**Galatians**		1:17	30, 72
10:11–15	70	2:16	77	1:18	121
10:12–14	77	2:20	58, 70	1:19	153
14:9	124	4:4	34, 54, 97	2:3	73
14:12	75	4:4–5	142	2:9	39, 68, 153
				3:4	129
1 Corinthians		**Ephesians**		3:13	73
1:2	77	1:11	73	**1 Thessalonians**	
1:17	173	1:15	77		
2:8	58, 143, 157	1:21	124	4:16	128, 129
4:4	75	1:22	73	4:17	130
8:4b–6	69	3:17	71	**2 Thessalonians**	
9:15	173	4:7–8	66		
10:9	28	4:8	61	1:7	128, 129
12:3	28, 69	5:25–26	74	1:7–10	75
15:20	121	**Philippians**		**1 Timothy**	
15:21	110, 119				
15:22–28	78	2:4–8	116	1:17	68, 73

2:5	126	7:25	127	2:22–25	111
3:16	39, 40, 110, 142, 152	7:26	112, 116	2:23	77
6:13–16	72	8:3	110	3:2	129
		9:14	98, 109, 113	3:5	113
		9:22	115	3:20	72

2 Timothy

4:1	75, 130	9:28	129	4:1–6	111
4:18	72	10:5	106	4:2	110
		10:10–12	110	4:2–3	142
		10:12	124	4:3	111, 169

Titus

2:13	29, 60, 68, 129	12:1–3	116	4:9	34
		12:23	62	5:1–13	70
		13:8	30, 72, 115, 126	5:5–12	111

Hebrews

1:1–3	27, 55, 58, 66, 68
1:3	30, 32, 33, 72
1:6	31, 32, 76
1:8	28, 68
1:10–11	30
1:10–12	29, 72
1:12	30, 75
2:7–8	124
2:8–9	114
2:10	105, 108
2:11–14	142
2:14	111, 115
2:14–17	99, 126
2:17–18	116
4:14–16	70, 115, 126
4:15	109, 112, 169
4:15–5:2	116
5:1	126
5:1–9	126
5:2	126
5:6	35, 92
5:7	109
5:8	58, 105, 108
7:17	92

James

1:13	109
1:17	72, 174

1 Peter

1:10–11	90, 95
1:11	93
1:19	113
1:21	116
2:22	113
3:18	105
3:22	124
4:1	105

2 Peter

1:1	68
1:16–18	53
3:2,18	28
3:12	128

1 John

1:1	24
1:1–2	40

5:20	29, 68

2 John

7,9–11	111

Jude

24–25	68, 73

Revelation

1:5	121
1:5–6	76
1:7	128, 129
1:8	29, 68, 71, 72
1:11	71
2:2,9,13,19	72
3:1,8,15	72
3:21	124
5:12	76
11:17	71
19:16	72
21:5	76
22:1	124
22:7	128
22:13	29, 71